Higher Education and Government

Higher Education and Government

An Uneasy Alliance

Edited by

W. Todd Furniss and David P. Gardner

AMERICAN COUNCIL ON EDUCATION   *Washington, D.C.*

Library of Congress Cataloging in Publication Data

Main entry under title:

Higher education and government.

    Bibliography: p.
    1. Higher education and state—United States—
Addresses, essays, lectures.   I. Furniss, Warren Todd,
1921–   II. Gardner, David P.   III. American Council
on Education.
LC173.H53   379.73   79-4028
ISBN 0-8268-1327-5

9 8 7 6 5 4 3 2 1

Printed in the United States of America

Contributors

WILLIAM G. BOWEN
Chairman, American Council on Education

WILLARD L. BOYD
President, University of Iowa

JOSÉ A. CABRANES
General Counsel and Director, Government Relations, Yale University

ALICE F. EMERSON
President, Wheaton College (Massachusetts)

CHARLES FRANKEL
President and Director, National Humanities Center

MARTHA FRIEDMAN
President, American Association of University Professors

JAMES M. FURMAN
Executive Director, Illinois Board of Higher Education

MARIAN M. HERSRUD
*Chairman, South Dakota's 1202-Planning Commission,
Department of Education and Cultural Affairs*

REATHA CLARK KING
President, Metropolitan State University

ALFRED M. MOYÉ
*Deputy Commissioner for Higher and Continuing Education,
U.S. Office of Education*

STEVEN MULLER
President, The Johns Hopkins University

LAWRENCE K. PETTIT
Commissioner of Higher Education, Montana Board of Regents

CORNELIUS J. PINGS
*Vice-Provost, and Dean of Graduate Studies,
California Institute of Technology*

FRANK PRESS
Director, U.S. Office of Science and Technology Policy

ALICE M. RIVLIN
Director, Congressional Budget Office

ROBERT M. ROSENZWEIG
Vice President for Public Affairs, Stanford University

C. ARTHUR SANDEEN
Vice President for Student Affairs, University of Florida

HERMAN B. SMITH, JR.
Chancellor, University of Arkansas at Pine Bluff

JOHN S. TOLL
President, University of Maryland

STEPHEN JOEL TRACHTENBERG
President, University of Hartford

MARJORIE DOWNING WAGNER
Vice Chancellor of Faculty and Staff Affairs,
California State University and Colleges

LINDA S. WILSON
Associate Vice Chancellor for Research, University of Illinois
at Urbana-Champaign

Contents

Preface

THE PAST FIFTEEN years have seen a rapid reorientation of American society, sometimes accompanied by civil disturbances but brought about chiefly by federal legislation and subsequent regulation and court action. To many whose lives are bound up with one or another of the stable institutions that are partners in the American "social contract," the reorientation has meant disorientation. In Yeats's words, they sense that "things fall apart, the center cannot hold." For those in higher education, the center is the autonomy necessary to provide society with teaching, research, and public services, rendered impartially and free from political or eccleastical restraint.

The planners of the 1978 annual meeting of the American Council on Education set out to explore the extent to which the responsibilities of higher education and government are now at odds, which ones each partner properly claims, and how conflict should be managed. The organization of this book reflects a fundamental premise: to do its job, a college or university needs the authority to decide about who shall teach, what shall be taught and how, who will be admitted to and graduated from an institution, what research will be done, and how institutional resources will be apportioned.

The twenty-two authors in this volume reflect many backgrounds and differing experiences, yet there is a large measure of agreement. That higher education needs considerable autonomy in making its internal educational decisions is asserted not only by the educators, but by other authors who see that the values of our pluralistic society—indeed its very pluralism—are best preserved by a minimum of government control. There is also agreement that government, representing as it ultimately does the will of the people, is within its rights in demanding accountability of all social institutions, including higher education. The distinctions to be made between control and accountability are, of course, crucial and draw the interest and comment of our authors. There is further agreement—surprising if one has been listening mainly to collegiate Cassandras—that things have not fallen apart, that the center can hold, that on balance government has maintained an appropriate restraint in its dealings with higher education, and that it does not wish or intend either to homogenize American higher education or to encroach on its established prerogative and independence.

Nevertheless, the authors are disquieted and concerned about certain trends, for in them they perceive some real and present danger to the higher education system. In the words of Robert Rosenzweig, "We are the victims of the least glamorous and most characteristic affliction of modern social policy—the unintended consequence" (see p. 93). Government's intentions—to achieve a just and economically sound society— are generally little different from higher education's. But the means by which government sometimes pursues its goals tend to threaten the fiscal and educational integrity of our institutions of higher education.

In a few instances when an outright attack on colleges and universities promised to undermine a fundamental academic prerogative such as the peer review system for decision making, the threat has been reasonably easy to turn away by a showing of the adverse implications associated with such heavy-handed efforts. To mount a defense against "unintended consequences," however, is a far more difficult and elusive task, particularly when the intention of the primary action is acceptable, as in the case of attempts to eliminate discrimination in access to or employment in higher education.

The authors offer us no single silver bullet to guarantee the survival of the "center" for colleges and universities, but they make many suggestions for reducing the threat to institutional autonomy. Beyond the value of the specific suggestions, however, is perhaps a greater value for the reader in observing good minds avoiding adversary rhetoric and coming to grips with the inevitable ambiguities that arise when our human institutions seek new and lofty goals.

Our debt to the authors is evident and gratefully acknowledged. We further wish to thank Martha E. Church and Frank Newman of the ACE Board of Directors and the staff members of our sister associations and ACE who helped plan the annual meeting. We also appreciate the effective work of Donna C. Phillips, who directed and coordinated the arrangements of the meeting.

W. Todd Furniss
David P. Gardner

1

Living with Change

Freedom with Responsibility

WILLIAM G. BOWEN

MARTIN TROW, director of the Center for Studies in Higher Education at Berkeley, tells the story of a fisherman at the turn of the century on the Isle of Aran, an island in the Atlantic to the west of Ireland. The fisherman was reflecting on his life and work, and he did so in these words:

> A man who is not afraid of the sea will soon be drowned, for he will be going out on days when he should not. But we do be afraid of the sea, and we do only be drowned now and again.

In our relationships with governments over recent years, I am sure that all of us have endured some sensation of drowning "now and again." And I suspect that most of us would confess to certain fears—or at least uneasiness—about where our relationships with governments may be heading, even as we recognize the importance of those relationships to our institutions and to the society that we serve.

This annual meeting has afforded a timely opportunity to assess some of our hopes and fears and to look ahead. In our working sessions and throughout the program, we have been challenged to identify those principles which we hold to be most fundamental; to consider ways to increase both understanding and cooperation among ourselves and with government; and to weigh various strategies by which we might achieve our objectives—remembering, with the fishermen, to choose carefully the days to go out.

On the basis of my experience as chairman of the Board of Directors of the American Council on Education, I am more convinced than ever that the Council, at its best, can reflect and mobilize the healthy diversity that is peculiarly characteristic of our system of higher education and that gives it a vitality and a creative independence unmatched in any other part of the world. I also want to say to you how extraordinarily fortunate we are, in my judgment, to have Jack Peltason as our president. He deserves all the help that each of us can give him.

In considering some of the rights and responsibilities that, in my view, we need to be prepared to assert and to accept, I want to begin with an unapologetic testimonial for our institutions of higher education and for the purposes we serve. I do so because the alliance between higher education and government is rooted, most fundamentally, in our capacity to make particular contributions to the general welfare which cannot be made as well—if at all—by any other set of institutions.

What higher education does

While there are innumerable ways of describing what we do, I think there would be broad agreement on certain basic points:
• Most obviously, our institutions have a major responsibility for developing the society's human resources—for work, for service, for informed citizenship, for self-fulfillment. Collectively, we offer a variety of forms of instruction, training, and education, up to and through post-doctoral levels of study, that is remarkable both for its diversity and its effectiveness. We seek always to educate new generations who will improve our understanding and correct our errors.
• Our institutions are also major centers of the scholarship and research which, as President Carter wrote to the Congress this summer,

> contribute in significant ways to our international trade balance, to productivity and economic growth, and to the solution of many of our social challenges.

• More generally and more fundamentally, colleges and universities are generators and incubators of new ideas, while at the same time conservers and transmitters of our cultural heritage. Aimed both backward and forward in time, we seek to revitalize and renew, as we also seek to preserve our inherited values and traditions. We are intrinsically schizophrenic, in that through our teaching and scholarship we celebrate the wisdom of our predecessors while simultaneously challenging old (and new) orthodoxies.

• Finally, many of our institutions contribute directly to the public welfare in and beyond our immediate communities.

Knowledge is our primary contribution, and in stressing its very general benefits to both individuals and the society at large, we should not hesitate to acknowledge its practical value as well. The *Washington Post* columnist George Will tells about the time when a town's electricity generator failed and various engineers were unable to fix it. So an elderly professor was summoned. He examined the generator carefully, then tapped it lightly once with a hammer, and power was instantly restored. He submitted his bill for $1,000.02 and itemized it: "Tapping—$.02. Knowing where to tap—$1,000."

Governments have recognized the critical contributions of colleges and universities by providing tangible support—over $22 billion of direct appropriations at federal, state, and local levels in 1976–77. In addition, our institutions have received substantial indirect financial assistance through the privilege of tax exemptions and through provisions of the tax code which stimulate private contributions.

But government's responsibility to higher education does not end with giving reasonable amounts of financial support. We also depend on government to protect our essential freedoms—from any individuals or other entities who may threaten them, and of course from government itself.

Let us be clear. In our kind of democracy, and given our educational philosophy, an environment conducive to the maximum possible freedom of thought and expression for each individual student and faculty member is critical to our ability to discharge our most basic educational responsibilities. This environment is not something that is merely desirable; it is essential. For the mysterious process of education to work well, we require a milieu in which every individual, whether the steadiest proponent of the majority viewpoint or the loneliest dissenter, is encouraged to think independently. In their dependence on this kind of environment for the achievement of their central purposes, our colleges and universities are different in nature from churches, labor unions, businesses, political organizations, social clubs, and essentially all other entities.

This freedom has not always prevailed historically and indeed does not prevail throughout the world today. It is well to remind ourselves (and others) of what can happen when universities become politicized. Many would agree that in recent years important educational values have been damaged or actually lost in countries as different as West Germany, Brazil, and the People's Republic of China when decisions on such key questions as admissions, appointments, and curriculum have been conditioned by considerations that are more political than educational.

Although periodically challenged and occasionally eroded to one degree or another in this country, our essential freedoms for the most part have been sustained, and they enjoy a statutory affirmation in such laws as the General Education Provisions Act of 1970, which stipulates that

> no provisions of any applicable program shall be construed to authorize any department, agency, officer, or employee of the United States to exercise any direction, supervision, or control over the curriculum, program of instruction, administration, or personnel of any educational institution.

Thus, in making their contribution to our alliance, those in government have a responsibility, in my view, not merely to tolerate the freedom of the academy, but to join with us in insisting on its functional importance—and then to exercise great restraint; to resist the inevitable temptations to become overly intrusive.

I also believe, and just as strongly, that societies can be expected to respect our freedoms only so long as we exercise them responsibly. This certainly does *not* mean that we should try to discourage criticism of government (or of business or any other group, for that matter); but we should be clear about our institutional obligation to be open to all points of view, as well as to encourage respect for evidence and a basic sense of fair play.

A kind of "social contract"

From my perspective, the legal prohibition against partisan political activity by tax-exempt organizations chartered for educational purposes represents just one manifestation of a much broader "understanding" between the academy and the larger society: We are given certain privileges, receive certain kinds of support, and are permitted important fundamental freedoms on the condition that as institutions we shall do our best to stand apart from contemporary controversies that are not primarily educational in character. This understanding can be seen as a kind of "social contract" in which we are homes for the critics, but not the critics themselves. Our strongly defended right to make our own faculty appointments, to make our own admission decisions, to shape our own curriculum—all of these hard-won prerogatives depend finally on our ability to persuade society that we are indeed firm and consistent in upholding our academic integrity and our commitment to an atmosphere which encourages a genuine diversity of views.

Of course, when issues of public policy are primarily educational in character, we must speak out institutionally: in these situations, we have firsthand knowledge and factual information to contribute, we have some special competence, and our voices must be heard if there is to be informed public discussion. But even here credibility and effectiveness require restraint—this time, on our part—speaking only when our institutional capabilities relate to the question at issue, and recognizing that our institutions as such (as distinguished from many individuals within them) have neither any charge nor any special competence to make judgments outside the fields of education and research.

Recognizing unique circumstances

When we do address issues—as varied as the nature of the tax code and provisions relating to mandatory retirement—we need to be willing to say what we believe and even to live with a certain amount of criticism that can come from arguing unpopular positions. I think we also need to be prepared to argue that, although we cannot always expect to receive hand-tailored treatment, we really are an odd set of institutions and in many cases laws and regulations designed for a broad array of entities will clash with our unique circumstances. We need to do our best to contribute to the achievement of important national objectives in areas ranging from equal opportunity to standards of safety and health. At the same time, we cannot be afraid to assert that regulations designed and enforced by those unfamiliar with our special characteristics may prove not only cumbersome, but damaging. When we do have a special case to make, we need to be prepared, without embarrassment, to make it. Just because it would be easier in many respects if all institutions throughout the society—or even all of our institutions of higher education—were the same, that is not the case, we would not wish it to be the case, and we should not behave as if it were the case.

One more comment is needed about *our* obligations. In addition to resisting pressures that would compromise our academic integrity— our openness to all points of view—and in addition to exercising some restraint in choosing even the educational issues which we address institutionally, we need to operate our own institutions responsibly and in keeping with general standards of accountability. It is right that instrumentalities of government, like other providers of support, be satisfied that their monies have been spent in accord with what we said we would do. In my experience, pressures for greater external controls often grow out of ineptness or irresponsibility on our part. Thus, I am a strong supporter of intelligent self-regulation, and of recognizing that claims for our freedom are debased, not advanced, when used to excuse slovenly procedures or judgments that cannot be defended.

I want to end these remarks by making an assertion and then recalling someone else's words. My assertion—I don't know how to prove it—is that the real challenges before us are less administrative than attitudinal. We need to improve attitudes on all sides, replacing the current presumption that is too often adversarial with something more akin to a sense of working partnership, in which each party respects the needs and understands the responsibilities of the other.

The words I want to recall are those of Frank Press, the President's Science Adviser, when he spoke to members of the Association of American Universities last October. In summarizing his own thinking about the relationship between higher education and government, he said:

> The university should remain a strong but fair critic of the government. But it should also be its best ally. We desperately need each other to deal with the very difficult problems that this country and the world face in the years and decades ahead. Only when the power of knowledge and forces of political action are united can most of those problems be solved. And others are bound to follow in their wake. So we are going to be working together for a long time.

That is surely so, and I retain a belief—call it a faith, if you will— that a reasonable mixture of mutual respect, shared commitment, good will, luck, and a sense of humor will get us more or less where we ought to be. The stakes are too great to allow a lesser outcome.

The Limits of Growth

ALICE M. RIVLIN

AS I thought of what I might say about the future of higher education and its relations, easy or uneasy, with the federal government, it occurred to me that I seem to have a recurring problem. Every ten years over the last two decades, like clockwork, a president of some entity has asked me to think about the financing of higher education, especially the role of the government therein. It has happened to me three times.

In 1958, President Robert D. Calkins of the Brookings Institution asked me to help him with a paper he had been asked to do on the role of government support for a symposium entitled "Financing Higher Education," edited by Dexter Keezer and published in the following year, 1959. I was very young then and his research assistant. My own role was minimal; I did "numbers for Bob," but it was my first exposure to this problem and it caused me to think about it and to start a project of my own at Brookings on the subject of higher education and the federal government.

Ten years later, I found myself as assistant secretary of the U.S. Department of Health, Education, and Welfare, and President Lyndon Johnson requested a study on federal support for higher education in his education message of that year.[1] I and a number of able colleagues put together a report that was published as the Johnson administration was leaving office in 1969.

Here I am again, ten years later, in 1978, with another president, the American Council on Education's Jack Peltason, asking the same question about the future of financing higher education and the availability of federal resources, constraints on these, and how things look down the road. Before we look forward, we should look back at some of these previous efforts to see from where we have come.

In looking back, it seemed to me there are two constants. One is that there is always an impending crisis in higher education. Its nature changes, but higher educators always view the future with dismay. We are always on the brink of a disaster which will shake the foundations of our system and threaten the quality of education.

1. *Toward a Long-Range Plan for Federal Financial Support for Higher Education: A Report to the President* (Washington, D.C.: Government Printing Office, 1969).

7

The second constant is that we, the higher education community, are always uneasy about our relations with the federal government. There is a basic ambivalence, which I think will not go away and probably should not go away. Higher education wants to be recognized for the important thing that it is; it wants support, but it always wants it in different ways from the federal government than the way it is getting it, with less bother. Despite all of which, life goes on in academia, decade after decade. Our very diverse system persists—large and small institutions, public and private. It goes on meeting different needs for what is loosely called higher education: students learn, professors teach and publish, football teams win and lose, Nobel Prizes are awarded, and somehow we muddle through.

One is struck, in looking back at the concerns of 1958, also by two themes: One was the quality of our education establishment, especially in science. Sputnik had been launched; the National Defense Education Act had just passed. The goal was to produce more technically trained people to help win the Cold War and more centers of excellence outside the traditional research universities and to stop the waste of talent. Waste of talent meant then that poor but able students often did not go on to higher education. In the rhetoric of the period, nobody was really concerned with their opportunities—it was the nation that was losing. We were wasting people.

Maintaining quality while expanding

The second theme, clearly, was the impending avalanche of students that was about to hit the universities. There was panic at the expected doubling of enrollments in the coming decade. There was going to be a need for buildings, for dormitories, for faculty. The big problem was going to be how to train enough teachers or attract them from other fields. This expectation coincided with the concern for quality: how were we going to maintain quality in the face of growing numbers? Concern existed also about the growing burden of federal research. So many organizations were turning to the universities for research; higher educators wondered how they could do it all.

A quote from Dexter Keezer's introduction to the volume in which Bob Calkins' piece appeared sets the tone of the period:

> Higher education in the United States is poorly financed at present. This is most strikingly attested by authoritative findings [which he does not

cite] that its faculty members—who are its most crucial element—are on the average only half as well paid as they should be.[2]

Faculty salaries are another constant in higher education. Probably faculty members are always about half as well paid as they should be, or so they believe. But,

> The present financial plight is only half the problem. The other half is created by the clear prospect of a doubling of the demand for its services over the next decade. Where there are about 3.6 million students in our colleges today, it is confidently to be expected that [there will be] at least 6 million in something called an institution of higher education ten years hence. Whether [he says direly] it will actually be such an institution in anything except name will depend in major degree on how well the job of financing is done.[3]

Wary of interference

This fear of impending doom in the face of the avalanche of students brought out, among other things, much hostility between public and private institutions. The suggestion was made frequently that resource needs might be met by raising tuition in public as well as private institutions—a suggestion that brought forth strong emotions and angry rhetoric. There was tremendous ambivalence about the federal government. Nobody in the higher education community had much experience with the federal government. There had been a long history of association but it consisted of specialized programs designed to deal with particular federal needs or matters: the land-grant colleges, the GI bill, college housing, war research. There was no policy of the federal government toward higher education nor did anybody think there ought to be one. The universities and colleges were looking for more support but were wary of it. Higher educators feared federal control; not just paper work and the aggravating regulations that perplex us now, but political interference with what was taught and by whom. Remember, this period was the McCarthy era, in which apprehension that somebody from the federal government might actually tell you what to think or what to say to your students was very real.

2. Dexter M. Keezer, ed., *Financing Higher Education: 1960–70, The McGraw-Hill Book Company Fiftieth Anniversary Study of the Economics of Higher Education in the United States* (New York: McGraw-Hill, 1959), p. 2.

3. Ibid.

Responding to crises

Ten years later, 1968, the concerns were different. The tidal wave of students had hit, college enrollments had in fact doubled since 1960, and they were expected to go on rising for at least another decade. Spending had gone up rapidly: total spending from 1.4 percent of the gross national product in 1960 to 2.3 percent in 1968, which is a whale of a rise. This avalanche of students had brought forth a burst of new federal programs, revival of the GI bills, the extension of social security benefits to college-age students, enactment of college work-study programs, government guarantees of student loans, graduate fellowships, and even a small fellowship program for undergraduates. But again, the response was ad hoc, comprised of a growing list of programs designed to meet the crisis of the hour. It was a growing and burgeoning time for all higher education and the federal programs came piling out helter skelter. These were mostly for things and for buildings, less for student aid, especially for undergraduates. There was no framework and no overall policy, for in an expanding universe, it is very easy to tolerate ambiguities and nonpolicy. Every claimant to support can be satisfied to some extent, and for a while nobody thought it mattered.

The search for a coherent policy

But by 1968, the costs of the Vietnam War meant slowing of growth in the rest of the budget, and the higher education community began worrying, quite legitimately, about the future as they were faced with continuing enrollment into the seventies. Higher educators were beginning to look for a coherent federal policy to help meet this new problem. But there were different ideas about what the federal policy ought to be. The events of the sixties—the civil rights movement, desegregation, the war on poverty, the agony on campuses especially of social reappraisal unleashed by the war—had focused attention on equalizing opportunity. Attention had shifted from the national waste of talent to the individuals' failures to achieve access to higher education and equality of opportunity. Research in the 1960s showed that high ability students from low-income families were about half as likely to go on to college as those from high-income families and only about a quarter as likely to go to graduate school. The reasons for this difference were not clear, but financial barriers appeared to be the key.

Equalizing opportunity

The federal focus was on equalizing opportunity and helping to maintain a strong and growing system, but the big question was how to do it. Strong emotions were invested in the debate over aid to students vs. aid to institutions. The public versus private split was still very strong and emotional. There were periodic outbursts of enthusiasm from various parts of the academic and nonacademic communities for schemes to raise tuition to full cost and require graduates to pay out of future income. It was in this atmosphere that President Johnson turned to HEW for a study of the long-range possibilities. We at HEW examined them all, and in the student vs. institutions split, we thought we had found an ingeneous solution, namely, both—student grants plus a cost-of-education grant to colleges. But clearly the burden of that report and other reports of the same period was on basic student aid with a heavy emphasis on the especially needy and opening access to colleges and universities. The report I worked on recommended basic grants of up to $1,500 per student, cost-of-education allowances to the institutions that took these students, a supplementary student loan bank, and so forth. Other reports on the subject were published. A number of legislative cooks were stirring the pot. Our report and others reflected an emerging consensus on the federal role and the result, as Ernest Boyer has noted earlier, was embodied in the higher education amendments of 1972, confirmed in 1976 and later: a strong federal commitment to equalizing education opportunity, equalizing access to higher education by providing student aid on the basis of need.

The commitment was not exclusive; the federal government has undertaken other types of programs and other major policies for higher education, but the 1972 amendments since that time dominated both the Office of Education budget and federal thinking about what OE does. This commitment appears to be well established and at the moment is not being questioned. Other concerns are being added to the federal things-to-fix list, most recently, the perceived plight of the middle- and higher-income people with kids in college. I have some personal sympathy for these parents (I am one of them), but it is not really clear why our lawmakers are so worried about us. If one looks at student charges as a percentage of after-tax income of families with eighteen- to twenty-four-year-old dependent children, one finds that this percentage has stayed remarkably constant. The incomes of these families have risen at about the same rates as those student charges. Other factors may be pinching these families' budgets: the "multi-child" phenomenon, whereby more families have more than one child in college. It may be inflation, not of the student charges themselves, but of other obligations to be paid out of parental budgets. It may be somehow a reduced parental willingness to support kids in college, especially in light of a perceived unfairness if aid is going to those with less income. But whatever is causing a resistance to college fees, it is there and I think we are going to hear a lot more about it over the next few months.

But here we are in 1978 looking back over a decade in which enrollment in higher education has continued to expand and in which spending has continued to grow absolutely and as a percent of the gross national product. A decade in which federal support for higher education has grown faster than the number of students, in which the major concentration has been on student aid but has also been on general growth in other aid from the federal government to higher education generally. Such support, excluding research and development support for students in institutions, in real dollars per student is about one and a half times as great now as it was ten years ago. But there have been costs of this giving—lots more regulations, lots more forms to fill out—real costs to be borne with the benefits.

The results of federal policy

As we look at the accomplishments of this period of growth—the long period of burgeoning higher education—I think we might first list survival of the diversity of the system; its mission has continued and it seems to be intellectually healthy. The financial situation is normal: that is, imperiled but not *in extremis*. It is about where one would probably expect the financial situation of higher education always to be. But what have the results been of the major federal effort, especially on equalizing opportunity? Have enrollment opportunities been equalized by reducing financial barriers? Unfortunately, not visibly. For the last ten years, the high school graduation rate of eighteen-year-olds has been about the same—it has been stuck at 75 percent. So the promise of a basic grant to help pay for college has had no apparent effect on high school completion. Nor has it had any demonstrable effect on the overall enrollment of eighteen- and nineteen-year-olds. That rate was 46 percent in 1965. It was 46 percent in 1972, and in 1976, and in 1977. It climbed as high as 50 percent in the late 1960s, fell as low as 43 percent in 1973 and 1974 (the first two years on which entering freshmen were eligible for a basic grant). It is very hard to make anything out of those numbers. The participation rate of twenty- and twenty-one-year-olds reached a high of 34 percent in 1969 and has ranged narrowly between 31 and 32 percent ever since.

The college enrollment rate for eighteen- to twenty-four-year-old dependents was 39 percent in 1971 and it still is. By income levels, things have not changed very much either. Eighteen- to twenty-four-year-olds from low-income families, the particular target of federal student assistance policy, achieved their enrollment peak of 25 percent in 1969. It has come down very slightly since then.

However, the big change has been that the black share of college enrollment has steadily risen and very substantially from 6.4 percent in 1968 to 10.7 percent in 1976 and 1977. Black college enrollment rates are still well below those of whites, but they are closer than they were, and the rates for Hispanics and other minorities are closing as well. But basically what we see is a constancy of graduation rates, of enrollment rates by income, or by anything else you can think of, except race. So what does this constancy mean?

It could mean that the perception we had ten years ago that financial barriers were keeping low-income students out of college was simply wrong or partially wrong, that there were other barriers, especially of motivation. That low-income students with enough desire for higher education ten years ago could go somewhere. They could get in, they could work their way through. It might be hard, it might be slow, but it was possible. That federal aid has made college-going easier, it has broadened the range of choice of institutions, but it has not basically changed the motivational factors. Blacks may be an exception, but even here one could argue that student aid need not have been a major factor, that affirmative action, that the lowering of job barriers, and the real and perceived improvement of posteducation opportunities for blacks could have explained the upsurge. But if one holds this view, it is not clear what policy prescription follows. One could say either forget student aid or keep it where it is because it does not do any good. Or one could say student aid by itself is not enough. There is a need either for larger sums, for a definite entitlement, so students know early in their high school career that they are entitled to go on to higher education if they have the ability, or for better high school preparation or guidance. Or this whole explanation may not be right. It may be that what we are seeing here is an instance of compensating factors, that student aid may have held enrollment constant through a period when they would otherwise have fallen due to a reduced perception of the value of higher education, surpluses of teachers, and unemployment of highly educated people. I do not think it is possible at the moment to assess this explanation, but my own view is that we have undertaken a national commitment to opening the channels of access to higher education through student aid on the basis of need, and there is not now in the federal establishment or anywhere else a disposition to question that basic commitment.

The certainties of demographics

What do we see as we look forward? I think two main factors will affect the future of higher education with respect to financing and the federal government over the next several years. One is a certainty and one is a probability. The certainty is that the number of people in the age group primarily served by higher education is going to decline substantially. Everybody who will enter college in the 1980s is already alive. Indeed, everyone who will graduate from college in the rest of this century, except for a few prodigies, is already alive, so we do not have to make any guesses about fertility rates. The class of 1999 has already been born. The demographic facts are these: the all-time high of eighteen-year-olds will come next year in 1979; there will then be a steady slide downward in their numbers until 1986, when there will be 18 percent fewer eighteen-year-olds than in 1979. By 1992, there will be only three quarters as many eighteen-year-olds as there are today and the number will stay level for the rest of the century. Not only will there be fewer people arriving at the traditional college age but their racial and ethnic composition will also be different from that of the 1970s. Blacks who are now 13.5 percent of eighteen-year-olds will be 15.6 percent by 1990. Hispanics will go up from 6 to 7 percent. Because of the momentum of history and the probable continuing association between parental education attainment and children's college-going rates, the changing composition of the eighteen-year-old age group tends to make it likely that enrollment rates will be lower in the 1980s. So, unless there is an upward change in enrollment or persistent rates in college of an unprecedented magnitude and speed, enrollments and graduations will fall. This outcome in itself may cause some offsetting movements. For example, the salaries graduates can command for their services may rise because there are fewer of them, inducing more enrollments as the perceived reward for higher education rises. The demographic changes are reasonably certain, but they will neither be abrupt nor catastrophic. The eighteen- to twenty-four-year-old population will go down from today's level, but in 1985 it will be about what it was in 1975, and in 1990, what it was in 1970. These are numbers that we have seen before. Higher education planners and policy makers should be able to cope with such significant shifts given the U.S. Census Bureau warning so far in advance. In addition, the problems that these trends suggest are in many respects the mirror image of the concerns of 1958. How to maintain the quality of students and faculty in the face of declining numbers? Will admission standards fall? Will faculties age? Will there be a place for young scholars?

The probabilities of rollback

The second factor, which I label less certain and which may well be transient though it will probably persist, is the increasing alarm of Americans at the size and complexity of government at all levels and the desire to reduce taxes and the share of the national product flowing through the government. We see these issues being debated in the states. I have been to California recently (and a more depressed group than California mayors is a little hard to imagine). I do not think that this government rollback is a California phenomenon, nor does the Congress of the United States. The desire to reduce taxes and government's size is a national feeling that, rightly or wrongly and whatever its reasons, we have had more government in quantity and in meddlesomeness than we needed for the last some years. This feeling may be both good and bad for higher education. I would suggest that higher educators may well be able to take advantage of this rising tide of sentiment among legislators to reduce the complexity of federal programs that affect higher education to get rid of some onerous regulations and unnecessary reporting. A constructive plan, I suspect, will get a hearing. One cannot just fuss. But the second consequence, of course, is that the higher education community cannot realistically expect large gifts from the federal government to make up the difference as other sources decline.

Federal politicians are hearing the same voices that everyone else is hearing in the state capitols and in other parts of the country. The rate of growth in the federal budget is quite likely to slow and competition for scarce dollars will increase from other programs, especially those that share a mission with higher education. An example is Concentrated Employment and Training Administration programs to improve employment opportunities; another is government and private laboratories competing for research funds. But like the demographic changes, any changes these competitions bring are unlikely to be abrupt. I would not suspect any substantial change or decline, but what is implied is that it is a mistake to feel that it is likely that any major new set of programs will be added to extend higher education's reach. Indeed, old programs will be very carefully examined at least for the foreseeable future.

Relieving a burden

Maybe this probable future is not all bad for academia. One could say that higher education is now relieved of the burden of expansion that seemed so heavy in 1958, that caused so much panic and so much anxiety about what one would do to maintain quality in the face of expansion. It will not be so necessary to be preoccupied with buildings, with recruiting faculty; it will be possible to concentrate on the business of education and scholarship. It need not imply stagnation; there is lots of room for change in education, for enrollments to change in type and in scope, for adults to move into higher education. There is no reason why scholars have to spend their whole life teaching; if the nation wants to support research and scholarship, it can do so. And it can do so in ways that will allow faculty members to move in and out of universities, thus solving the problem of what to do with new scholars. It can be normal—even more than it is now—to move between higher education and government and research institutes.

The higher education community can expect more scrutiny of performance of government-supported programs, more skepticism about new spending, but I think no reversal of basic commitment. Based on past performance, one can expect some moaning and groaning and viewing with alarm over pared down support and latitude, but one can also expect our resilient system to muddle through. We have been through what would logically seem to be more difficult times than this when academia was being challenged to grow rather than consolidate. Somehow, I think we are going to make it.

My only hope is that some other president asks me to look at higher education and the role of federal government in 1988 so that I get another chance to see whether my forecasts were right.

2
Who Shall Teach?

Academic Freedom and Retirement

MARJORIE DOWNING WAGNER

AN EXAMPLE of higher educators' concern over the effect of certain kinds of legislation on our colleges and universities is the recent history of California statutes affecting mandatory retirement. In any unhappy contest over which of us may be afflicted the most by legislative actions that intrude on the management of our universities and colleges, we must feel in California like the rueful "winners." Hundreds of bills are introduced each year in the California legislature that directly or indirectly bear on higher education. There are bills assigning responsibility for grading, bills determining academic holidays, bills giving students places on faculty promotion committees, bills touching, in short, on every facet of university governance and management. Many of these bills are passed. We in the universities must then live with new statutes that too often are ambiguous, or worse, damaging.

The first California legislation amending existing statutes on mandatory retirement came about as suddenly as did the passage of comparable federal legislation during the summer of 1977. While we were aware that AB 568, authored by Assemblyman Richard Alatorre, had been introduced early in 1977, the same political instinct that kept the higher education associations in Washington from at first actively opposing the retirement bills as they were moving through the Congress was working in us. Our governmental relations staffs recognized that relaxing restrictions on the age of retirement was an idea whose time had clearly come, and warned that opposition from us might adversely affect the interests of the higher education community in the long run. The bill was also being supported by the governor.

Nonetheless, in the few remaining days before the session was to close in August 1977, the University of California and particularly the independent colleges and universities began frantic last minute efforts to amend the Alatorre bill. They were unsuccessful. The bill was unanimously passed out of the assembly and passed out of the senate by a vote of 28 to 3.

AB 568 was signed into law on September 16, 1977, with an urgency clause making it effective immediately. For the California State University and Colleges (CSUC), the effect of the law was to amend the retirement law already in effect for the Public Employees Retirement System and the State Teachers Retirement System to provide that employees who reached the mandatory retirement age of 67 and who wished to continue in active employment be allowed to continue subject to certification by the employer of their competency in their positions. Authority to establish rules and regulations governing the determination of such competency was provided to the board of trustees of CSUC as well as to the regents of the University of California, the state personnel board, and city and county governing bodies for employees under their respective jurisdictions.

A companion bill, AB 586 (Alatorre), was also signed into law. This bill extended to employees in the private sector the right to continue in employment beyond the normal retirement date provided the employee demonstrates the ability to perform the functions of the job adequately and the employer is satisfied with the quality of work performed. This bill also adds a new labor code section which makes it an unlawful employment practice to refuse to hire or employ, or to discharge, dismiss, reduce, suspend, or demote any individual over 40 on the grounds of age except when the law compels or provides for such action and in other specified circumstances.

In November 1977, the CSUC board of trustees granted authority to the presidents of the nineteen campuses in the system to provide temporary certification to the Public Employees Retirement System or the State Teachers Retirement System that an employee might continue in employment beyond the mandatory retirement age of 67 until such time as rules and regulations were adopted. The board continued at this time the existing trustee policy covering executives and certain academic leaders (such as deans) who serve at the pleasure of the trustees and whose assignment normally terminates at age 65 unless continued at the discretion of the trustees.

Certification of competence

Meanwhile, the Chancellor's Office of Faculty and Staff Affairs and the Statewide Academic Senate, made up of elected faculty representatives from all the campuses, struggled with the problem of "certification of competence." The implications for tenure of such a requirement were immediately apparent to faculty and administration. So were the implications of affirmative action efforts to appoint greater numbers of women and minorities, and for the increasing concern for institutional vitality in the prevailing condition of "steady state." The difficulty of establishing a workable procedure for review of faculty members who had attained the age of 67 but who wished to remain in employment was perceived as a nearly insurmountable barrier to ever retiring such persons at all. This likelihood had to be contemplated in the context of other factors such as the increasing numbers of faculty with tenure on all campuses, the low rate (3 percent) of turnover of those tenured faculty, a median faculty age between 45 and 50, the diminishing number of new faculty positions throughout the system as a result of little or no growth in enrollment, and limited resources for faculty development. Institutional renewal under all these circumstances looms as a problem of the greatest importance.

As these problems were being confronted in California, the federal legislation was moving swiftly through the congressional maze with the fight for exemption of tenured faculty members from the new retirement age attracting the full attention of the higher education community. In the midst of uncertainty about the possible effect of whatever the final federal legislation might be, the debate in the California state university and colleges system was centering on the rules and regulations for certifying competence rather than on the age of mandatory retirement.

In effect, by requiring certification, the statutory age of 67 was eliminated as indeed was any age for mandatory retirement unless the evidence of incompetence became overwhelming.

An abandonment of tenure

There was agreement that the review process for certification after the age of 67 would parallel the process used for retention, tenure, and promotion with peer review and recommendations to the president of each campus. The question, however, of "burden of proof" became controversial at once. With dismissal for cause the only way for tenured faculty to be released, except for financial exigency, there were those who contended that the university must demonstrate a faculty member's incompetence in the certification process rather than the converse. Others, including the Statewide Academic Senate, proposed a new status for faculty continuing beyond the age of 67, "post-tenured." Persons in this category would retain only some of the rights and privileges of tenure, such as service on significant university committees, but they would lose their seniority in the event of possible layoff. The reasoning behind this rather extraordinary abandonment of tenure was complex, but at its heart was the deep faculty repugnance for "post-tenure review." The process of certification most assuredly introduced the concept of the review of tenured faculty to determine whether or not they should be retained, with the judgment to be based on their "competence in the position." The opposition to such a concept is based on principle, of course, but it also is colored by reluctance to judge the competence or incompetence of tenured colleagues.

The agonizing discussions continued throughout the winter and spring of 1978. Meanwhile, the federal legislation setting mandatory retirement at the age of 70 was passed with the temporary exemption for five years of tenured faculty members. This political compromise offered no relief to California institutions of higher education facing certification, although the difference in the age of mandatory retirement between 67 and 70 caused new legislation to be introduced that would align California law with federal law. Thus, senate bill 130 (Deukmajian) was adopted in August 1978, and becomes effective on January 1, 1979. This law amends the Public Employees Retirement System law by raising the mandatory age of retirement to 70. It continues, however, the onerous requirement of certification of competence for employees who wish to continue beyond the age of 70.

Cleanup legislation

During the summer of 1978, yet another bill (AB 3646) was introduced by Assemblyman Alatorre as a form of "cleanup" legislation for his original bill. The University of California was successful in having an amendment to this bill introduced which allows the university to take advantage of the temporary exemption for tenured faculty in the federal law. The regents' retirement system is not covered by the laws requiring certification for members who wish to continue employment beyond the mandatory retirement age, and thus the University of California is not troubled by the problems facing the California State University and Colleges with respect to certification.

In order not to jeopardize the bill, the Public Employees Retirement System, of which almost all CSUC faculty are members, opposed amendments suggested by our system. The University of California has a relatively small number of faculty (fewer than 100) who are members of the Public Employees Retirement System. In view of the opposition of the Public Employees Retirement System to an exemption for certification of faculty, the university did not seek an exemption under that system. Instead, the university sought and won an amendment to the law covering the University of California Regents Retirement System (which includes the balance of their faculty) allowing the university to continue to require members of that retirement system to retire at age 67 until the expiration of the exemption provided for tenured faculty members under the federal law (July 1, 1982). The CSUC was unable to secure such an amendment.

The Alatorre cleanup legislation has, moreover, complicated the certification requirement even further as it applies to faculty members. The reference to competence has been deleted from the bill and for it is substituted the term "eligibility," defined as "job performance of standard or above." While such a designation is customary for nonacademic and civil service employees who are evaluated periodically against a list of uniform performance standards, it is highly inappropriate for the complex evaluation of faculty based upon delicately balanced variables like teaching ability and creative and scholarly achievement. What, in short, is "standard" teaching performance? How is it to be evaluated?

Yet another bill

In a united effort to rescue the CSUC from the thicket of these legislative entanglements, the trustees and the faculty have determined to seek relief through yet another bill. The legislation to be sponsored when the legislature comes back to session in January will return the system to the conditions prior to 1971: mandatory retirement of academic employees will be required at age 70, with the option by the campus to continue the employee on a yearly basis, without requiring certification.

Opposition to such a bill is to be expected because it grants a special exemption to CSUC academic employees (including librarians and student affairs officers as well as instructional faculty). We must depend on the same arguments for such an exemption as those used by the American Council on Education and other associations in their approach to the Congress. Laura Ford has summarized these well.[1] For one thing, it must be made clear that with the bulk of our faculty, hired during the expansion of the 1960s, unlikely to retire before the end of the century, and with a virtual standstill in new faculty hiring because of declining enrollments, very little turnover can be expected in the coming years. Inducements for early retirement are being developed, but inflation is a deterrent to those who might otherwise elect such plans. If we are to have any degree of institutional flexibility to respond to changing student needs, and if we are to have any degree of continuing institutional vitality through the appointment of younger persons and better ethnic and sexual "mix," we must have the option of retiring faculty members at the age of 70.

More crucial is the matter of certification. Ford cites the notorious difficulty of determining when a tenured faculty member's performance has declined to such an extent that proceedings "for cause" are warranted, and points out how exceedingly rare such proceedings have been. She reminds us that the difficulties inherent in academic evaluation processes are unrivaled in other professions. The requirement for "certification of eligibility" for academic employees over 70 under the new California law would create in the coming years such problems of morale, to say nothing of expense and time, as to make it virtually impossible to retire anyone at any age short of visible and demonstrable senility. And even then?

Thus, the struggle with mandatory retirement legislation inappropriate to higher education in California goes on. We in the CSUC (faculty,

---

1. "The Battle Over Mandatory Retirement," *Educational Record,* Summer 1978, pp. 204–23.

administrators, and board members) are working unanimously to retain insofar as possible our freedom to determine for ourselves *who shall teach,* for the benefit of the people of the state who look to us to provide quality education now and in the future.

Defending the Power to Appoint

JOHN S. TOLL

THE ISSUE of who decides who is appointed to the teaching faculty has been carefully explored for many years as the current procedures have developed in colleges and universities. It is especially important to protect the appointment procedures of our major universities, for there are people who wish to force appointments that do not meet the standards of academic excellence under the universities' own processes of determination. When external pressures may attempt to alter the decision or to misrepresent the issues involved, the academic community should be alert to defend our processes of appointment.

The appointment of faculty and academic officers is one of the most weighty responsibilities of a university president. As president of the State University of New York at Stony Brook for the past thirteen years, I carried out the responsibility for appointments that was assigned to me, approving some recommendations and rejecting others. I am similarly considering carefully each appointment that it is now my responsibility to make as president of the University of Maryland.

University appointment procedures begin in the academic department, where candidates are initially selected, usually after a careful search. The department recommendation for one or more candidates for any given position is then reviewed at various levels, and the decision of whether or not to make the appointment is then made after careful review by the president or other designated official. This process gives reasonably fair assurance that quality will be preserved, that a common standard will be used in determining appointments throughout the university, and that the appointments will be based on the qualifications of the candidates for the position involved. The appointment procedure is important to our system of academic rank and academic tenure. The granting of academic tenure is especially important in American universities, for tenured professors then have protection to teach and to conduct research according to their own best judgments. The preservation of academic freedom and academic excellence depends very much on our system of appointments and academic tenure and upon the public confidence in our systems.

The process of recommendations and selection of faculty members is usually kept confidential until the final appointment is announced. This protects the individuals involved, as well as the institutions. As a result, many members of the public are not fully familiar with the process. Thus, many outsiders do not realize exactly what the process is or that many recommendations do not lead to actual appointments. For example, at one of the nation's best universities, with faculty of high quality that can be expected to maintain an extremely high standard in their recommendations, in recent years about 10 percent of the department recommendations for tenured appointments in the arts and sciences of that university have been refused by the president.

Each stage of the appointment review process should be serious and should never be considered pro forma. It is through close insistence on academic standards in these various reviews and through extensive communication among academic officials and department members that a university's standards for academic appointments are maintained.

Making the appointment decision

Even though almost all the details of the appointment selection and review process are usually kept confidential, there are occasionally cases when disputes arise within the university which then become public. The discussion in such a case may center on issues that are not appropriate to the consideration of an academic appointment. The appointment decision should be based on the candidate's qualifications for teaching and scholarship and for the specific duties involved. Such matters as the candidate's personal beliefs, political opinions, or religious convictions are irrelevant. To the extent that such issues become part of the debate, the public begins to discuss a different decision than the one that is actually before the university. Outsiders can then begin arguing over whether or not certain political beliefs should disqualify one for appointment in the university; of course, a person should be eligible for consideration for a university teaching position independent of political beliefs, but the individual should *not* be given a university appointment just because of political beliefs. The judgment as to whether the academic appointment should be made should be based on a total assessment of abilities to teach and to perform other responsibilities of the academic position. Since the public often does not have information sufficient for an informed judgment of these qualities, the debate on irrelevant issues may be misleading. It is important for the members of the academic community in such a case to insist that the proper standards be maintained and to resist any attempts to force proposed appointments that have been rejected by the university in accordance with proper academic criteria and procedures.

When I became president of the University of Maryland on July 1, 1978, I found several recommendations for academic appointments awaiting my consideration. Under the bylaws of the Board of Regents of the University of Maryland, it is the responsibility of the president to appoint all faculty members of the ranks of associate professor, professor, and professor and chairman. No recommendation for such an appointment nor offer of an appointment constitutes a commitment of the university unless and until it is approved by the president. I acted on each of the pending recommendations as rapidly as I could, consistent with my other responsibilities and with the necessary consultation and careful review in each case.

Deciding not to appoint

One case involved an associate professor with permanent tenure at another university. He was being considered as a candidate for a position as professor and chairman at the University of Maryland. I decided after careful review *not* to approve this recommendation. My decision was based on my judgment of the qualifications of the candidate for the particular appointment. This was not the first case of those pending before me last July that I decided not to approve, but it was this case which attracted the most public attention. Unfortunately, public discussion has tended to confuse the actual decision with other issues.

Even before this recommendation reached my office, a dispute had arisen within the department over the wisdom of the recommendation, and this dispute had become public. The acting governor of the state had responded to repeated press inquiries for comment on the case and then several newspapers overreacted to the governor's comment in editorials, some of which recommended that the appointment be made. The difficulty was that the candidate's political views became a public issue. I have often appointed individuals who hold political views similar to those of this candidate in the past, but based solely on their academic qualifications. Any candidate who is an associate professor at one university could be promoted at any time to the higher rank of professor at his or her own university or could be considered for an appointment at higher rank at another university, but he or she has no right to demand an appointment at another university just because of his or her political views.

Threatening academic freedom

The unfortunate aspect of the disputed appointment at the University of Maryland was that many of those who were urging an appointment felt that they were defending academic freedom, when in fact they were trying to force upon the university an appointment that had been refused in accordance with the university's own procedures; such attempts to pressure a university either for or against an appointment are clearly a threat to academic freedom and not in support of it. This type of case illustrates the need to defend regular university procedures and the desirability for those outside the university to avoid hasty judgments about university decisions.

In weighing the qualifications of the candidate to see if he was the best qualified person that we could reasonably hope to find for this post, I reviewed the file that had been assembled. I also invited all of the senior faculty members at the rank of associate and full professor in the department to meet with me. Most of them were able to attend this meeting, where there was a full and frank discussion of the appointment. In addition, both those attending the meeting and those unable to attend were invited to submit written comments to me, which were extremely helpful.

Opinion regarding the appointment within the faculty was split. The majority of the responding associate and full professors favored the appointment of the candidate, but over one-third of them recommended against the appointment; this opposition included most of the senior department members who had previously served as chairmen of the department and were thus in the best position to judge qualifications for this appointment. I found many of the comments at the meeting helped in evaluating the qualifications of the candidate for this post.

I also sought other expert advice on a confidential basis. It was only after such consideration that I decided not to make this appointment.

There has been wide public discussion of this proposed appointment, both before and after my decision and both for and against my decision, but much of this discussion focused on issues that are not appropriate. For example, some persons have said that they felt I should approve the recommendation, even though it was not merited, because others might believe that the appointment had been refused on account of the candidate's political beliefs. I must stress as clearly as I can that appointment decisions at the University of Maryland are not and shall not be based on political beliefs, but shall be based on the qualifications of the candidate for teaching, research, and appropriate service.

Strengthening a free society

Our nation is dedicated to the principle that all points of view can be presented, and this openness should be especially true on a university campus. Our democratic society is strengthened by the free expression of views and by our willingness to tolerate and to examine all ideas and viewpoints. Not far from here, in the nation's capital, is the Jefferson Memorial, with Thomas Jefferson's famous oath carved around the cupola: "I pledge upon the altar of God eternal hostility against every form of tyranny over mind of man." These words of Thomas Jefferson should guide the spirit of a great university. I am firmly committed to making the University of Maryland a forum where all views can be freely presented and examined. But, we do not have to alter our normal standards of appointment to make clear our toleration of various political opinions.

Some people who have agreed that this candidate was not the best qualified person for the post have nevertheless urged that the appointment be made because of the editorials that had been written in major newspapers in support of it or the indications that national organizations might criticize the university if the appointment were not made. A university must be willing to stand up firmly to such outside pressures. On March 24, 1969, when there was outside pressure on me concerning faculty appointments at Stony Brook, I issued a statement that included the following paragraph:

> Figures from outside the University who undertake to substitute their judgment for academic due process imperil the integrity of the University and the historic principles of academic freedom. Such actions immediately and inevitably endanger the essential rights of advocacy and

inquiry which have distinguished great universities for hundreds of years. These University traditions are essential to maintain both excellence and order within the academic community.

I feel as strongly in support of these words today as I did when I first issued them. I urge those from outside a university who are tempted to pressure a university to make any particular appointment to examine the damage they may bring to the university by their interference in its regular processes and also to ask themselves on what basis they are making their judgment. Are they really using the proper criteria to determine whether a particular candidate is the best qualified for a specific post? Have they consulted with experts in the disciplines in other universities and asked them if they had a similar position for professor and chairman recently open and, if so, who were the leading candidates for such a position?

Defending academic standards

One person has said that, although in his judgment the candidate did not have the qualifications in teaching, scholarship, and administrative ability that one should seek for this post, he was tempted to recommend the appointment to avoid the threat of a legal suit. Academic administrators must have the courage to defend proper academic standards against all forms of outside pressure. In my opinion, it would be just as wrong to give in to the threat of a legal suit as to any other outside pressure.

Although there was considerable pressure from outside the university for this proposed appointment, mostly from people who had not examined the candidate's qualifications, I viewed such pressure as irrelevant in reaching my decision. To the best of my ability, I based my decision on my evaluation of whether or not the proposed candidate was the best qualified person we could reasonably hope to get for the particular position.

One other aspect of this entire case deserves mention. An important element of a university's appointment procedures is a careful appraisal of a candidate's qualifications. Such a judgment requires input by experts, who normally will give their opinion most frankly if their views are protected by confidentiality. Thus, most universities assure confidentiality to their informants in order to gain balanced appraisals of candidates.

The American Association of University Professors, however, has demanded that the University of Maryland detail its reasons for rejecting the candidate in question. It is not the policy of most major universities to state the reasons why particular candidates from outside the university are not appointed. For example, this is not the policy at the distinguished university where my fellow panelist, the national president of AAUP, now holds appointment. It is clearly inappropriate for the AAUP national office to demand detailed reasons from the University of Maryland when most other major universities do not give reasons for rejecting outside candidates.

When the University of Maryland, on advice of counsel, did not comply with the AAUP request, the AAUP, over the university's objections, sent an investigating team to the university. The actions of the national office of the AAUP in this case have been contrary to the interest of academic freedom. In light of these actions, the academic community must find a new national organization which will take over the role of protector of academic freedom which AAUP occupied in the past; I hope that the American Council on Education and other responsible organizations will give some thought of how such an organization can be established.

Universities must defend their current procedures for careful review of candidates' qualifications and for decisions by the presidents or other designated officers. Outside pressures may endanger academic freedom and should be excluded to the best of our abilities. In this way, we have the best chance of seeing that we preserve academic freedom and do indeed choose those who are most fit to teach.

Collegiality in Changing Times

MARTHA FRIEDMAN

AS HUMANKIND begins to learn a little about the physiology and psychology of intelligence and the learning process, many aspects of the environment finally are seen to influence access of individuals to education and hence to the opportunity to participate in the process by which successive generations are educated. We cannot today concern ourselves with this sifting of individuals through the structure of society or through the structure of the higher education system. We must deal instead with the finished candidate about whom a decision must be made and with the system by which that decision is achieved. Recognition that decisions are shaped by social policy expressed in law is understood in this discussion.

My purpose is to ask and attempt to answer several questions: Who should decide who teaches? To what extent does legislation or other government regulation intrude on decisions? What can we appropriately do to avoid a degree of intrusion which is intolerable or harmful to the continued functioning of our colleges and universities?

There seems to be agreement throughout the higher education community that ideally those persons who are capable, through knowledge and experience, should and must decide who will perform the teaching, research, and service functions in colleges and universities. Under this scheme, those persons who are capable are faculty in the disciplines and academic administrators, that is those administrators whose primary function is to run the instruction and research programs of the university as distinct from its nonacademic processes. The choice of those academic administrators is itself a part of this system of decision making.

A concise articulation of this system of collegial decision making appears in the *Statement on Government of Colleges and Universities,* jointly formulated by the American Council on Education, the Association of Governing Boards of Universities and Colleges, and the American Association of University Professors:

> Faculty status and related matters are primarily a faculty responsibility; this area includes appointments, reappointments, decisions not to reappoint, promotions, the granting of tenure, and dismissal. The primary responsibility of the faculty for such matters is based upon the fact that its judgment is central to general educational policy. Furthermore, scholars in a particular field of activity have the chief competence for judging the work of their colleagues; in such competence it is implicit that responsibility exists for both adverse and favorable judgments. Likewise there is the more general competence of experienced faculty personnel committees having a broader charge. Determinations in these matters should first be by faculty action through established procedures, reviewed by the chief academic officers with the concurrence of the [governing] board. The governing board and president should, on questions of faculty status, as in other matters where the faculty has primary

responsibility, concur with the faculty judgment except in rare instances and for compelling reasons which should be stated in detail.[1]

This description of collegiality, or shared authority as it is often called, reminds us that decisions on such matters should originate in the academic department where the most precisely informed judgment can be brought to bear, and that such decisions should be reviewed by those of ever-broader competence. University officers most remote from informed judgment are, in this system, constrained from substituting their own judgment except upon extraordinary occasions. This system is considered to be desirable because it is designed to produce the most competent decision, and it is competence which is an eventual goal of academic institutions.

Variations in collegiality

If we agree, generally at least, that this definition is of the ideal system, can we say with any assurance that that is how decisions are invariably made? The answer must be no. Studies of governance systems usually conclude that practice varies from institution to institution and from time to time, but that usually some elements of collegiality exist always. Some of us have encountered situations in which virtually no decisions have been made, so that a person may achieve tenure without his or her knowledge or that of the department chair. Or faculty may be virtually excluded from participating in tenure decisions. These are of course extremes. Usually, the shared authority model of governance functions at least to the extent that some consultation is provided between department faculties and administrators.

Elements common to a well-working collegial system must include: (1) the identification of appropriate groups to participate in the decisions; (2) stated criteria by which faculty are to be judged and specification of how the criteria are to be applied; and (3) a defined route for appeal of, or additional consideration of, adverse decisions.

Each of these elements is subject to legal constraints as well as academic custom. In the first instance, state law routinely assigns to a college or university governing board the legal authority and responsibility to employ faculty, as do the charters of private institutions. While the sharing of this authority is based on consent, it proceeds in law

1. *Policy Documents and Reports* (Washington, D.C.: American Association of University Professors, 1977), p. 43.

through the protection of the due process and free speech rights of individuals. The construction and application of criteria are limited by federal and state statutes that prohibit inequitable treatment of individuals on account of age, sex, religion, race, or national origin. The integrity of these procedures is to be further guaranteed by a well-defined method for considering complaints arising from decisions. Such procedures are required by Title IX of the 1972 higher education amendments.[2]

Collective bargaining

With the onset of collective bargaining in higher education some ten years ago, it was believed that such a process would inevitably destroy the ability of faculties, administrators, and governing boards to share authority for decisions. That view was seldom held by unionizing faculty who more often than not sought to organize their colleagues for the purpose of insuring their own participation in academic governance as a contractual right. Governance questions are and will continue to be a major focus of the tension of faculty-administrator relations as they always have been. Joseph Garbarino has said that the availability of collective bargaining to all faculty in the private sector and to some in public institutions has strengthened established senates and spawned new ones on unorganized campuses.[3] Continued insistence on the necessity of faculty participation in personnel and other decisions is a manifestation of this vigorous interest in collegial governance, which is bound to intensify because of adverse economic conditions, if for no other reason. Many observers agree that this interest in decision making will be maintained whether collective bargaining or a more traditional governance structure is employed to achieve participation.

In law, collective bargaining is not mandatory. But if entrance to the process is discretionary, adherence to regulatory laws is not. Among the issues raised by higher education collective bargaining, three are central to the continuation of the collegial system:

Definition of the bargaining unit. Are faculty who participate in per-

2. Grievance procedures are described by W. Todd Furniss in "Grievance Procedures: A Working Paper" prepared for the Commission on Academic Affairs, American Council on Education, 1975.

3. Joseph W. Garbarino, "Collegiality, Consensus, and Collective Bargaining," in *Collective Bargaining in Higher Education, Proceedings, Third Annual Conference* (New York: National Center for the Study of Collective Bargaining in Higher Education, 1975), p. 14.

sonnel and other policy decisions properly protected by the National Labor Relations Act and other legislation? Until quite recently, the configuration of bargaining units to include all faculty except for the occasional exclusion of department chairpersons could be said to be the rule.[4] Other questions such as geographic and occupational scope of the unit have seemed more manageable through the application of community of interest and ease of bargaining rules. If the greatest benefits to higher education is to be achieved through the process of collective bargaining, it seems certain that the Feller/Finkin standard must be met:

> It is imperative that the faculty's governance constituency coincide with the constituency that selects a bargaining agent if there is to be a satisfactory accommodation between the two.[5]

Scope of negotiations. Commonly used language defines "wages, hours, and other terms and conditions of employment" as subjects for negotiation. The issue turns upon the question of negotiating governance practices under the rubric "other terms and conditions of employment."

A substantial portion of the writing on higher education bargaining deals with governance, as do many rulings of employment relations boards. Most faculty bargaining agents insist that if governance mechanisms cannot be written into the contract, the purpose of bargaining is defeated. Some administrators and members of governing boards are equally insistent that the incorporation of shared authority procedures and practices into the contract represents an intolerable intrusion into the exercise of legal responsibility specified by statute or charter; that is, such an agreement is offensive to or violative of management rights.

These issues are accessible to resolution. One response has been to regard governance issues as a permissible subject of negotiation. Reasonable persons can then write a contract which regularizes relations so as to avoid violation of the rights and responsibilities of each party to the agreement. Legislation can be written to preserve both the collegial structure of universities and the legal responsibilities of governing

---

4. The recent decision of the second circuit involving Yeshiva University raises a fundamental question for private sector collective bargaining which remains to be settled through additional judicial review or legislation. The court declined to enforce an order against the administration on the grounds that the designated faculty were managerial employees under the terms of the Act.

5. David E. Feller and Matthew W. Finkin, "Legislative Issues in Faculty Collective Bargaining," in *Faculty Bargaining in Public Higher Education* (San Francisco: Jossey-Bass, 1977), p. 111.

boards. Or governance issues may become the topics for "meet and confer" agreements rather than more formal negotiation.[6]

The use of third-party arbitration in grievance resolution. A common feature of collective bargaining contracts is a formal grievance procedure designed to facilitate the settlement of conflicts of various sorts. Third-party arbitration is not an unusual final-step feature of grievance procedures.

Earlier in this decade, it was often predicted that the use of arbitration in academic decisions was likely to occasion the most sweeping of changes in higher education. That belief was founded on the apprehension that grievance procedures would be written which would provide for the submission of professional decisions on retention, promotion, and tenure to arbitrators outside the institution. Such an eventuality would sacrifice not only the legal authority of the governing board but also the ability of faculty and administrators to make decisions crucial to the health of the institution.

This problem has been avoided in the design of grievance procedures by the use of several devices. Contract language may exclude questions of professional judgment from the scope of the grievance procedure. Procedural questions only may be admitted to the process. Alternatively, arbitral activity may be limited to procedural questions and professional judgment eliminated. Or, the contract may prescribe the establishment of a panel of academics from within the institution to arbitrate when a difference between professional judgments arises.

Analytical research on the course of arbitral experience is sparse, making it difficult to assess the efficacy of the several approaches to academic arbitration. Generally, most contracts in four-year institutions presently exclude substantive issues from arbitration; the possibility of substitutions of judgment, in the arbitral award of tenure for instance, seldom arises.

Results of arbitration

One effect of the resort to arbitration in four-year institutions seems thus far to have been salutary in tightening up decision procedures, an outcome also brought about by the existence of grievance procedures in nonbargaining institutions. Many see as less beneficial the increased

6. See the discussion of scope of bargaining in *Faculty Bargaining,* pp. 117–41.

formality of faculty-administrative relations, which has made these more expensive and cumbersome.

During this decade, participants in the higher education enterprise have experienced at an accelerating rate changes in the system of relationships by which decisions are made in other areas of academic administration and management. Some of these changes have occurred as a response to internal institutional needs or desires and have been designed to further institutional autonomy. Most have resulted from the activities and requirements of agencies external to higher education or at least external to the institutional setting. Whether these changes are the result of individual initiative or collective compulsion, the results have been mixed, and the goodness or badness of change are traceable to both sources.

Integrity of process

If it is true that a majority of us in the academic community believe that academic decisions must be made by those most competent to make them, then we must find the means by which to maintain the integrity of that process. It has not always been maintained in the past, nor is it universally maintained presently.

Often, the emergence of new approaches to problem solving underscores the inadequacies of previously valued devices. For example, despite our distaste for the increasing litigiousness of faculty over the past decade, the effect of much of that litigation has been to secure First Amendment rights, among other things, to those of us who have chosen to be teachers. So, too, may the process of reaching agreement, which we call collective bargaining, secure to the academy a degree of protection which might not otherwise be achieved from external intrusion. That can only be accomplished if the responsibility to guarantee that security is accepted by both the parties. Such protection cannot be accomplished any other way, which has ever been the case.

3

What Shall Be Taught?

Curricular Decision Making

LAWRENCE K. PETTIT

SOCIETY has an obvious stake in the educational process, particularly at it relates to transmission of cultural heritage and imparting the knowledge and skills essential to intellectual discovery and improvement of the human condition. Yet the very essence of education requires that those who have knowledge (rather than public officials) are best able to determine what is worth knowing, what is likely to be known, and what can and should be taught. It is not necessarily the prerogative of the academy, however, to determine what is in the public good, government officials being vested with that charge.

The inevitable tension between those decision makers responsible for public policy and those who are responsible for the creation and transmission of knowledge reflects a clash of perspectives that may alarm us on occasion, but should not surprise us. This tension exists at all levels of government. Here, I will examine the forces affecting decisions for public higher education at the state level. In setting the agenda for higher education a decision maker acts in accordance with one of two competing models, depending on what values he or she regards as most relevant to the higher education task.

These two models are normative, because they describe essentially the clutch of values and assumptions that persons carry with them as they approach the task of education policy making. I am suggesting that one's values and assumptions, however vague and inchoate they may be, will roughly fit one of these two models.

The first is what I call the *public interest* model. This model takes as its starting point the responsibilities of the state to its people. For example, the state's responsibility for the health, welfare, and safety of its citizens results in mandated curricula in such fields as drug and alcohol abuse and control. The state's interest in the education of its youth leads to legislated certification requirements for public school teachers, which in turn mandates certain parts of the teacher-training curriculum. Or the state's concern for social engineering—redressing socioeconomic inequities and providing equality of opportunity—leads to mandated curricula about or for minority groups. In the same vein, a legislated open admissions policy, requiring state institutions to admit all graduates of accredited high schools within the state, is an indirect interference with curriculum in that the legislature is saying to institutions of higher education, "You will devote considerable resources to remediation, whether or not you are budgeted for it."

The dynamic of the public interest model is political, reflecting what political scientists call "the authoritative allocation of values for a society," or "the distribution of rewards and deprivations." In the American setting, the character of this dynamic is roughly democratic, based on the assumption that the interplay of forces in the political arena will result in compromise decisions approximating what is best for society as a whole. This model, in its pure form, does not recognize the logic of expertise, or the reality that some opinions are worth more than others.

The second model is what I call *epistemic*. The basic assumption of this model is that those who have knowledge (however it may have been derived through education, revelation, or whatever) know best. In its purest form, this is a model of modified corporatism, providing justification for the existence of independent social structures whose decision making is virtually untouched by the requirements of public policy. Organized religion obviously fits this model, but in a lesser degree, education and the self-regulating professions would also fit.

In addition, I would propose that there are at least three other decision models that do not relate so directly to the basic values that the participants bring with them to the game, but rather, to how the game is played. These I call "bureaucratic," "political," and "professional."[1] Under the first two, decision making is highly centralized; under the third, it is more decentralized.

The bureaucratic model

Under the *bureaucratic* model, decisions are made predominately by central administration—either on-campus or in the central office of a multicampus system—or by governing boards or statewide coordinating commissions. In unusual (and unfortunate) cases, this model could even include a state department of education. Direct political interference by the legislature is minimal, although it is possible for the governor to assert himself through one of these structures, particularly a coordinating commission. This model assumes a weak (but not necessarily incompetent) faculty. However, political pressure groups have very little influence as the bureaucratic decision makers function with a high degree of independence and insularity.

The *political* model assumes that it is the duty of the faculty to teach, of the administration to manage, of governing and coordinating boards to plan and budget, and that the broad policy-making prerogative, even as it respects curriculum, rests with public officials. Thus, under this model, the legislature mandates curriculum, and establishes broad academic policy for public colleges and universities.

The *professional* model is the classical model of faculty autonomy. The faculty sets the curriculum without interference from anyone else.

Four decision arenas

The interaction of the various models for determining what is to be taught occurs in four decision arenas. In the legislative arena, the style of decision making is political with a public interest rationale. This is

1. This typology, which apparently is derived from Max Weber's classical discussion of authority patterns, is borrowed from Burton Clark's discussion of patterns of coordination and planning in higher education in a presentation by him at the 25th Annual Meeting of the State Higher Education Executive Officers Association in Savannah, Georgia, August 1, 1978. I had considered propounding a fourth empirical model, the market model, also a part of Clark's typology. The assumption of this model is that students vote with their feet, and thereby determine what colleges and universities teach. I rejected the notion that this is a model of the same dimension as the other three, however, on the grounds that (a) market considerations are probably never exclusive of other considerations, and (b) market considerations such as these are intervening considerations in *all* other models, no matter which set of decision makers has the effective authority to determine curriculum.

the most open and participatory arena of the four, but also the one in which curriculum decisions in all likelihood are the most threatening to the integrity of higher education. We would expect both organized interest groups and fleeting constellations of angry or concerned citizens to exert their maximum influence here. In addition, students are beginning to learn that they can secure from legislatures concessions which they could rarely expect to receive from faculty, administrators, or governing boards (for example, student representation on the governing boards themselves). It is not unrealistic to expect, therefore, that organized students will increasingly turn to legislatures to codify their curriculum preferences. Similarly, when curriculum decisions are made by legislative bodies, there is an inducement to enterprising faculty members to guarantee high enrollments in their own disciplines through legislative edict, at least if they represent disciplines (such as political science, economics, or history) where such requirements remotely make sense as a matter of public policy.

There are many problems, of course, with legislatively prescribed curricula. One of the most obvious is that decision making within the legislature is decentralized so that those who wage the battle for a mandated curriculum are not always involved when critical appropriations decisions are made. Seldom, therefore, does added money accompany the added burden of legislated curriculum. The other obvious problems are first, that highly technical decisions are made by persons without any apparent expertise and second, setting academic policy in response to political pressures leads to instability and uncertainty, and can render chaotic the process of planning a student's academic program.

Decision-making authority located in coordinating boards on the one hand, and governing boards or administrators on the other are the next two decision arenas. The bureaucratic mode would characterize the process for both; public interest would underlie decisions by coordinating boards and epistemological justifications, decisions by governing boards or administrators. In proposing this typology, I view coordinating boards as closer to political decision makers and farther removed from campus decision makers than are governing boards. I would suggest that a coordinating board serves primarily the governor or legislature, or both, with a strong public interest orientation. Clearly, the staffs of coordinating boards have greater academic orientation than do other state employees, on the whole, and are generally able to interpret higher education to the political branches, and vice versa. Nevertheless, they are distinguishable in background, style, and perspective from the staffs of governing boards. In some respects, neither governing board staffs nor campus administrators fully accept coordinating board staffs into the academic fraternity. Coordinating boards are perceived as functioning more in the bureaucratic orbit, and less in the academic orbit.

Campus advocates

Governing boards and their staffs, in contrast, tend to be closer to the campuses and generally are more enthusiastic advocates of campus interests in the political arena. They, unlike coordinating boards, usually have a high degree of autonomy from the political branches, often based on constitutional provisions. I would suggest that even *statewide* governing boards, while viewed as more remote from campus interests than are institutional boards, nevertheless retain an essential academic quality, and attract and recruit as their executive officers the kinds of persons who would be very much at home as campus presidents. They come down on the side of the campus, rather than the elected representatives of the public, and therefore approach curriculum in the normative mode of the epistemic model, rather than the public interest mode.

From the faculty point of view, it probably makes little difference whether mandated curricula come from the president of the institution, a governing board, coordinating board, or the legislature. In any of these cases, the locus of decision making is external to the sacred precincts of the professoriate. For that reason, curriculum decisions made by, or unduly influenced by, boards carry with them a basic problem also associated with legislatively prescribed curricula: a lack of legitimacy in the eyes of the faculty.

Faculty control

Faculty senates and comparable entities are the fourth decision arena. Epistemological justification, in the professional mode, colors decisions made under this pure academic model; faculty control over what is to be taught is unquestioned. Fortunately, this well-guarded faculty prerogative has remained inviolate at most institutions of distinction. That the principle of faculty autonomy is violated on occasion is probably a bad thing, but we need to reserve judgment on the results of such incursions. As the faculty collectively and ponderously exercises its will, it is not always responsive to the public interest. At what point the faculty should compromise academic considerations for the public interest is doubtless an unsettled question, even within academia, and we should not expect an easy or abiding consensus. Yet there is some truth to the old maxim that college and university faculty are the most liberal people in the world about everyone else's business, and the most conservative about their own. If modifying the curriculum to respond to changing social needs is viewed as desirable, then the Byzantine workings of faculty self-governance must be viewed as exasperating.

Two other decision arenas are possible under the typology described here. One would be a legislature comprised mostly of college and faculty members. Decision making would be political and based on epistemic considerations. A more likely possibility would be a faculty senate, functioning in the professional mode, deciding issues in the perspective of the public interest model. In such instances, faculty would make the decisions respecting curriculum, but considerations of social justice and public need would outweigh academic criteria. These possibilities are unlikely because I cannot imagine an on-going decision-making structure which would typify either set of circumstances.

Institutional autonomy

This typology formalizes what admittedly in the real world is a messier and less structured pattern of decision making. But formal models have utility usually in giving us standards against which to evaluate what we observe and in helping us formulate questions. When we discuss the question who determines what is to be taught, we are discussing essentially a matter of institutional autonomy. But how do we define institutional autonomy? Is it faculty decision making, irrespective of the wishes of the administration or the trustees? Or does the president speak for the institution, even in those cases where he has not consulted the faculty? And does the right of his administration to make decisions for the institution therefore constitute institutional autonomy? How about the governing board? The board is responsible for the institution's well-being and longevity. Does the board's prerogative of setting policy for the institution irrespective of, or even contrary to, the wishes of public agencies constitute institutional autonomy?

At what point does representation of institutional interest break down? It seems to me that if a governing board assumes the normative baggage of a coordinating board it may flatter itself for its public interest orientation and protection of taxpayers' interests, but in so doing it can be charged with abandoning its trust and leaving the institution naked on that battlefront where politics and academia intersect.

My purpose here has not been to evaluate. I have intentionally ignored any discussion of which model is "right" and which is "wrong." Surely there is value in both orientations. How do we balance those two sets of values, and which decision-making arena is best able to bring about that balance? I suggest it will require more time and space to answer those questions conclusively, but they ought to be posed regularly and subjected to rather structured, formal inquiry.

Curriculum Development by Evolution

ALICE F. EMERSON

AFTER a decade or so of relative dormancy, the undergraduate curriculum has become a major issue on the campuses of many United States colleges and universities. Left almost entirely to the forces of supply and demand over the last ten years, the curriculum has undergone explosive changes; enormous numbers of intensely specialized courses have been developed and students have had virtual freedom of election in choosing among them.

The publication of the Carnegie report, *Missions of the College Curriculum,* and the publicity given the Harvard core curriculum proposals during the spring of 1978 are perhaps the most visible evidence of renewed interest in what is taught.[1] Recent writing has focused on two general issues: (1) the substance of the curriculum—what should be taught? and (2) the sources of influence on the curriculum—who and/or what shapes curricular decisions?

Discussion of curricular content has been largely focused on the con-

---

1. The Carnegie Foundation for the Advancement of Teaching, *Missions of the College Curriculum* (San Francisco: Jossey-Bass, 1977).

cept of general education and the need to recreate a common intellectual experience through a core curriculum. Reinstitution of requirements and efforts to focus on the integration of knowledge and broad-based approaches to teaching and learning have been put forward in direct opposition to overspecialization and what Grant and Riesman have described as "disenchantment with the over-optioned life."[2]

Related to this central issue is another concern, namely, an interest in giving renewed attention to value questions and issues of moral and ethical consequence. Like the last wave of academic requirements, efforts to address value questions all but disappeared in the late 1960s. Recognizing that they neither could nor should stand any longer *in loco parentis,* many educators suffered a failure of nerve in approaching value questions from any perspective at all, expressing the view that ethical and moral questions were beyond the appropriate purview of the academic enterprise. A recent resurgence of concern over issues ranging from Watergate to DNA research to questions of medical ethics has added both urgency and legitimacy to educators' efforts to reinstate consideration of moral issues and value questions in the formal curriculum as well as in the community life of colleges and universities.

A third substantive curricular area receiving particular attention now is that of basic skills. New programs are being proposed and instituted to address the need for increased English language and quantitative skills among our student population.

Recent discussion of the consequences for the curriculum of outside influences has highlighted pressures relating to the job market and those emanating from government. In addition, as conventional financial resources become less and less able to carry the costs of higher education and new funding sources must be developed, some educators have expressed the fear that the curriculum may be directly affected. The question has been raised, for example, if corporate support is sought and received in much greater measure, will the treatment of American business in the curriculum and the training of women and men to enter the business world be altered?

The dynamics of decision making

The current flurry of institutional activity regarding what is to be taught and the worry about curricular integrity in the face of pressure from

2. Gerald Grant and David Riesman, *The Perpetual Dream: Reform and Experiment in the American College* (Chicago: The University of Chicago Press, 1978).

outside forces has led educators and others to question the dynamics of the curriculum decision-making process. What are the major forces that sustain and change course offerings and academic requirements? While the locus of final formal decision making as to what shall be taught is internal to institutions—largely in the hands of curriculum committees and faculties—the interplay between external forces and internal decision making is constant and significant.

Historically, forces external to education institutions and beyond the control of administrators or faculty members, namely, social and economic needs, have provided the major incentives to the development of higher education. The training of ministers and the preparation of physicians and other professionals were principal examples in the seventeenth century, and the training of men for republican citizenship was added to the list of social needs after the Revolutionary War. The development of the education of women closely parallels the evolution of their position in American society. The training of teachers was followed by training for nursing, librarianship, and social work after these fields emerged as acceptable occupations for women during the nineteenth century. More recent examples of the response of the education community to social and economic needs would include the particular attention given to black studies and computer science during the late 1960s and early 1970s and the enormous expansion of scientific training following the advent of Sputnik a decade earlier.

The ideal and reality

In addition to social and economic needs of the society, the availability of funding and the sources from which monies may be obtained have great impact on the nature of curricular development, particularly in times of financial stress. Tension between the ideal of academic freedom in teaching and research and the realities of the need for financial support has long been an operative aspect of the American higher education scene. Clearly, the availability of support influences both research projects submitted for funding by faculty members and curricular projects for which institutions as a whole seek funding. The problem of fashion and the demand for innovation and newness by funding sources is not a new phenomenon, nor is it more characteristic of one funding source than another. The interests of individual philanthropists, the missions of various foundations, and the programs put forward by the federal government all reflect biases to which education institutions must be responsive if they are to be the beneficiaries of financial support.

A third force beyond the control of contemporary educators influencing what shall be taught is individual institutional history and mission which provide the contemporary and basic future parameters within which curricular choices may be made. The evolution of an institution's mission generally reflects a continuing dialogue between an educational ideal and the practical necessities of the times. In times of financial stress, particular contemporary worries may be the dominant force in setting curricular direction. Present concern about enrollments and funding have resulted in greater emphasis on "consumer" interests than was the case a decade ago. Attracting, retaining, and satisfying students has led to greater emphasis on work place needs and the development of programs that will respond to the changing roles of women as well as new student constituencies. Lifelong learning is seen as a potential offset to the decline in the numbers of eighteen- to twenty-two-year-olds, and efforts to create a special distinctiveness in programs are the result of intensified interinstitutional competition. While the list of potential external influences on the curriculum is very long, it is clear that only a few are of determinative importance at any given time. In a period such as we are experiencing now, the stakes for many institutions are inordinately high. Enrollment and funding are issues of survival for some and retrenchment and stringency for almost all. In such a climate, practical considerations tend to dominate and the degrees of freedom for curricular change initiated and carried out within an institution are very limited. While the leadership of the national education community can perform an important role in articulating, sifting, and legitimizing directions for development and change, factors internal to institutions preclude more than a tinkering at the margins just now.

Declining faculty turnover

The most important internal force in determining what will be taught is the composition of the faculty. As turnover declines and the steady state sets in in greater measure, curriculum designers will, of necessity, be forced to propose only those courses which can be taught by existing faculty members. While faculty development programs will allow some retraining, the status quo will carry enormous weight. Curricular change in the near term will more likely be reflected in the courses students elect to take rather than in the catalogue offerings as a whole. Greater emphasis will also likely be placed on learning experiences that are not part of the traditional formal academic program.

New money from outside funding sources can have a major influence on new curricular developments in the next decade. Many contemporary educators fear that in seeking and spending such money, major distortions may be introduced into the academic enterprise. How can we assess this fear? How can we predict what impact on the curriculum such external forces may have?

We can examine curriculum committee and faculty meeting minutes and we can study successive catalogues, taking note of additions, deletions, and substitutions and try to correlate these with identifiable influences on the institution. We can make connections between availability of research funding, graduate student training trends, and the teaching interests of faculty members in subsequent generations in an effort to trace the evolution of funding biases. We can review the stated objectives of foundations and government granting agencies to see whether or not money was made available for purposes related to the curriculum and, if so, whether or not there is a correlation between funding availability and curricular development in institutions.

Little fundamental impact

A thorough review in any or all of these areas would, in my judgment, lead to two clear conclusions: (1) there is a demonstrable influence of the availability of funds on institutional curricular development, and, (2) the central core of the liberal arts curriculum—the major areas of study and disciplines that form the basis for the organization of the curriculum—has not been substantially affected by outside pressures. Some new courses have come into being as a result of the availability of outside funds (the basic writing course at Wheaton, funded by the Fund for the Improvement of Postsecondary Education, is an example), but for the most part these new courses have been added to the periphery without much impact on the fundamental curricular structure.

During the decade of skyrocketing enrollment, new courses were added with relative ease. In addition, pressure from students to drop requirements, provide relevance in the curriculum, and maximize freedom of choice had more impact on curricular change than government programs or other funding source interests. While acceptance of government funding has brought with it several intrusions by government into other areas of institutional life, the direct impact of the government on what shall be taught in our colleges and universities is relatively insignificant. The current wave of consumerism is likely to have a more far-reaching impact that the academic community will have much greater difficulty resisting.

A review of the forces affecting the curriculum cannot be confined to those for which a visible trail or catalogue record exists. Decision making occurs also in the form of inaction. Thus, omission is also a critical aspect in determining what will be taught. Omission may be overt and purposeful or it may be by oversight. Without a lobby, a tradition, a social or economic need, a particular relationship to institutional mission, or a mentor, there is no way for an area of study to get on the list of curricular concerns. An area of study that was unwanted, threatening, or viewed as unimportant by a majority of institutional curriculum makers would surely be denied consideration, leaving no record for review. The nonprovision of research funds and the nondevelopment of teaching materials relating to the activities, contributions, and thinking of women in every discipline is a clear example of curricular omission. Whether by oversight or design, a decision by nondecision took place so that the study of women was not included in what was (or is) to be taught.

An examination of the curriculum-making process in a broader framework produces a striking parallel between decision making in the area of the curriculum and decision making in the contemporary democratic system in America. Clearly, the curriculum is the result of a multiplicity of influences. Those that are dominant at any given time are those most closely related to the particular societal and educational issues of the day. A multiplicity of groups and interests exert varying amounts of pressure through whatever means are available. Sorting and sifting of these pressures occur both beyond and within institutions; the result is that by the time issues are framed for actual debate and decision by faculties, the range of choices is very modest. The outcome of the process must be practical; that is, it must satisfy major institutional constituencies. Students must be attracted, not repelled, by the curriculum and must elect courses in sufficient range so as to spread the teaching load among departments and faculty members. Funding sources, both public and private, must also be willing to supply the resources necessary to support the enterprise.

The rules of the game

Process is the critical focus in the evolution of what will be taught, not substance. As in political decision making, the participants are those who care about the outcome and are in a position to exert influence. The views of those with greater resources will receive greater weight; interests that are unorganized and have no means of being heard—for example, proponents of research and study about women—will not be included. The "rules of the game" will apply and, if followed, the assumption will be that what results is both good and legitimate because process is the only test. Even in education, there are no basic operative tenets. There is no agreed upon common goal or set of values which the curriculum must meet.

The virtues of decision making rooted in process are not inconsequential: openness is maximized; risk is minimized; the result is likely to be that which satisfies the largest number of constituents; and the process is "democratic." The major weakness of this decision-making scheme is that little leadership and almost no planning are possible.

The answer, then, to the question, who decides what is to be taught, is those who engage in the dialogue—those who have an interest in the outcome and sufficient clout to be influential. Whether this is as it *should* be is another question.

Institutional Autonomy and Curricula

WILLARD L. BOYD

EQUALITY of opportunity is the foremost goal of our times. The right of an individual to an education is stressed today. Education opportunity should always mean access to superior education.

The quality of higher education depends upon the creativity of individual faculty members and students. We live in a pluralistic society which recognizes that there are many valid answers to the various questions we confront in education. Through institutional autonomy and academic freedom, we assure diversity and individuality.

The basic responsibility for curriculum is vested in the faculty and academic administration of America's colleges and universities. That public responsibility is both individual and group. Each faculty member is constantly making curricular decisions. These individual decisions are not made unilaterally but, rather, in concert with departmental and collegiate peers to meet the needs of students and the public.

It has been said that with greater democracy comes greater bureaucracy; yet, bureaucracy is the antithesis of democracy. The aim of a democracy is to decentralize, not centralize. This aim is as valid in today's complex society as it was in the rural America of 200 years ago. No single group or agency can effectively or efficiently design and administer in detail programs for every college and university in the nation. Educational diversity and individual initiative should be cultivated, not stifled. In the name of planning and efficiency, the cry is, "When in doubt, centralize." If American education is to remain vital, the cry must be, "When in doubt, decentralize."

This philosophy was espoused by Mr. Justice Powell in the *Bakke* case when he reaffirmed Mr. Justice Frankfurter's concurring opinion in *Sweezy* v. *New Hampshire.*

> It is the business of a university to provide that atmosphere which is most conducive to speculation, experiment and creation. It is an atmosphere in which there prevail "the four essential freedoms" of a university . . . to determine for itself on academic grounds who may teach, what may be taught, how it shall be taught, and who may be admitted to study.

Nevertheless, centralizing forces are eroding this decentralized responsibility for curriculum. In the name of professional standards, consumer protection, and public accountability, governmental and private bodies increasingly are enacting laws and promulgating regulations which affect instruction. These external pressures range from influence to control. They constitute a major threat to educational diversity.

Traditionally, our federal government has not engaged directly in making education policy. It has done so indirectly only in limited ways and for specific purposes in conjunction with federal spending. This involvement has taken the form of fiscal support for particular fields, but usually has not included curricular intervention. Recently, however, Congress has sought to predicate funding on curricular change. Thus, health capitation funds have been available only if there were programs in clinical pharmacy, community dentistry, and family medical practice. To complicate matters further, some of these governmental intrusions into curricula have actually been invited by segments of the academic community, intent upon promoting a particular interest.

Regulations and stipulations

Similarly, the executive branch has taken action which affects curriculum. Most prominent is the current regulation of the Veterans Administration, which stipulates that veterans' education benefits will be based on contact hours, to the detriment of independent study. Health sciences training grants have sometimes altered curricula by being narrowly restricted to certain specialties or by requiring interdisciplinary relationships which are not necessarily appropriate. Examples are the highly specialized programs designated in the Health Professions Educational Assistance Act of 1976 and the National Institutes of Health (NIH) National Research Service Awards Program. It is not possible, for example, for a dental college to apply for a Teaching Expanded Auxiliary Management (TEAM) grant or a medical school to apply for an Emergency Medical Service (EMS) training grant unless the college is willing to accept in all its particulars the specific program endorsed by the federal agency.

In addition, the federal government is now setting general college and university policies and procedures in areas of legitimate social concern. Unfortunately, federal methods sometimes lead to unsound education policies and procedures. An example of improper federal means were the initial proposed regulations implementing Title IX of the 1972 higher education amendments, which contained provisions designed to eliminate sex stereotyping in texts. These provisions were omitted from the final regulations as improper curricular incursions.

A willingness to intercede

The judiciary has been reluctant to intercede in educational curricular matters. Ordinarily, the courts have limited their decisions to issues of procedural due process concerning the appointment and termination of faculty and staff and the dismissal of students for disciplinary reasons. Courts continue to acknowledge that the judiciary generally lacks the expertness to evaluate academic decisions. Nevertheless, courts remain willing to intercede where academic decisions are arbitrary, capricious, or in violation of the contractual relationship between student and school. Increasingly, courts are called upon to respond to complaints that the quality of academic programs is not as advertised; that fair notice of academic requirements was not given; that the value of the education provided was misrepresented. In a society increasingly concerned with redress of consumer grievances, recourse to the judiciary will continue.

In our federal system, the state has the basic authority to charter and authorize postsecondary education institutions. To the extent that government has been involved in curriculum, it has been principally at the state level. Through the years, there has been a remarkable forbearance by all branches of state government with respect to postsecondary curricular matters.

This attitude has changed recently with the emergence of line item budgets and coordinating boards. For the most part, state action pertains only to public institutions, but in some cases, independent institutions are affected also. State coordinating boards have acted to eliminate curricula deemed unnecessarily duplicative. In making such decisions, these boards and their staffs have made judgments on curricular specifics. Moreover, state coordinating boards have identified new education needs of the state's population. This attention has led to the establishment of particular programs with particular curricular orientations.

A threatening uniformity

A basic threat to institutional autonomy currently exists in the programmatic uniformity which specialized accrediting agencies seek to impose upon colleges and universities. Too often, specialized accrediting agencies emphasize the narrower interests of discipline in the context of the broader college or university. Their advocacy of specialization must always be balanced against the ultimate value of general education to the specialist in a changing world. The professions and society have greatly benefited from the inclusion of professional studies on collegiate and university campuses.

At this time, specialized accrediting agencies constitute a greater threat than the government to institutional curricular control. No accrediting agency should promulgate requirements which require educational uniformity. Professional faculty and students must also be free to learn and to experiment. The growing need for public accountability can be met without imposing uniformity on all programs. Specialized accrediting agencies, like regional accreditation, should develop general guidelines pertaining to educational quality and permit different approaches to common objectives of quality.

An instrument of public policy

In recent years, the federal government has become involved in accreditation. Most notably, the Office of Education of the U.S. Department of Health, Education, and Welfare now recognizes accreditation as sufficient evidence of educational quality to establish institutional eligibility for federal funding. The authority of the commissioner of education to recognize accrediting agencies for this purpose has been relied upon to impose required standards of accrediting agencies on the institutions they accredit. In effect, accrediting agencies are becoming instruments of public policy as determined by the Office of Education.

An example of the extent to which these policy concerns range is found in the deliberation of the Office of Education's Task Force on Futuristic Criteria for Recognition of Accrediting Agencies. The chair of that task force considers the effectiveness of education in terms of social benefits, fiscal cost control, and the responsiveness of post-secondary education to the demands of its constituents as the proper concern of USOE in recognizing accrediting agencies. In addition, many state governments are looking to professional accreditation as evidence of educational quality to permit graduates to seek professional licensure.

Society's significant influence

Probably the most significant external influence on postsecondary curricula today is society in general. Liberal education is under its greatest attack in American history. For those of us in the academic community who believe in basic education, it is later than we think.

The public is becoming increasingly convinced that basic skills are not as valuable as applied skills. Applied skills are equated with specific rather than general education. Liberal or general education is caught between disciplinary parochialism and vocational pragmatism.

To assert the value of liberal education is not to deny career education. Rather, the value of liberal studies lies in their lasting superiority in preparing the individual for changing needs of life and work. Oversimplified, the purposes of general education are to teach the student to analyze, to synthesize, to comprehend, to explain, and to act ethically. Younger people face an average of six job changes in their lives. It is misleading to indicate that a job awaits at the end of any given curriculum. The availability of work is determined in large measure by the state of the economy, which because of its constant fluctuations defies accurate prediction. Of course, we need vocational, technical, and professional education. But we also need general education. The unpredictability of the future argues for a more general educational process which continues through life. From the sound base of general education, new information and new skills, indeed new careers, can be secured through on-the-job training and continuing education.

If we are to strengthen general education, we must convince the faculty, students, and public of its basic value.

Institutional autonomy and academic freedom are consistent with public accountability and responsiveness. Colleges and universities in this country have been sensitive to the changing needs of society. Indeed, they have often been at the forefront of change. They have been an integral and important part of every period of this country's history. In their individualized instruction, they have capably exercised a public trust. They must continue to have flexibility which will permit diverse responses to changing conditions. This diversity can be accomplished in numerous ways:

1. *General guidelines*

Where there is a legitimate governmental or accreditation objective, multiple institutional responses should be permitted. A case in point is Title IX, where each institution establishes its own plan for compliance. Similarly, in the case of specialized accreditation, accrediting standards should be broadly conceived and applied so that curricular changes can be anticipated and encouraged. Rigidity in governmental regulations and accreditation standards creates a consistency and symmetry that may be highly valued by its creators, but it smothers the vigorous thought and inquiry so critical to vital education.

2. *Horizontal coordination of postsecondary institutions*

It is desirable to encourage voluntary horizontal cooperation regarding curricula among all postsecondary institutions within a state. Where possible, this should extend to voluntary regional cooperation. In this way, educational problems of duplication and other curricular concerns can be addressed by those best equipped to deal with them—the institutions themselves.

3. *Self-regulation*

Professional and institutional codes of conduct can clarify the responsibilities of faculty and institutions. Traditionally, maintaining these codes has been a role played by the American Association of University Professors in developing model faculty policies. The American Council on Education has recently sponsored the development of a Code of Fair Practice.

In adopting voluntary codes, it is important that their purposes be understood and the consequences anticipated. Voluntary codes should focus on general objectives, rather than on the specific means of obtaining them.

4. *Consultation*

It is imperative that there be an open-ended, open-minded consideration of curricular needs with students, staff, governmental agencies, accrediting agencies, alumni, the professions, and the public at large. In doing so, it should always be made clear that advice is being sought and that the ultimate responsibility for the curriculum remains with the faculty and the academic administration.

In these ways, we place the responsibility for equal opportunity for quality education on the faculty and the institutions. This requires more than our rhetoric. It requires our action. By a steadfast commitment to institutional autonomy and academic freedom, American higher education will have the wherewithal to meet and adapt to the never-ending frontier of education.

4

Who Shall Study?

In Support of a Social Ideal

C. ARTHUR SANDEEN

IN 1899, my grandfather came to this country from Sweden. He was twenty years old, and had eight years of formal schooling. After settling in Northern Wisconsin, he met a young Swedish girl who had worked her way over to the United States. They were married in 1904, and, by 1914, they had four boys. Two of them went to the University of Wisconsin, one to Minnesota, and one to Carleton. I found an opportunity to ask my grandparents, when they were almost 90, what it was about this country that caused them to come and what they felt best about in their lives. Their answer was simple: In America, they felt they had a chance. Here, hard work and high aspirations could result in a better life for them and their children, and the vehicle to get there would be higher education. The idea that a common laborer from Sweden and his wife could send their children to college, and did, still seemed like a miracle to my grandparents in 1967, and it provided them with perhaps the greatest personal satisfaction in their lives.

Nothing is unique about this story. It has been repeated literally millions of times, and I suspect many higher educators are direct beneficiaries of similar situations. I relate this story, however, without apology. We are still engaged in the most exciting and worthwhile human experiment in history. We are serious in this country about our efforts to make access to the good life not a function of who one's parents are, where one lives, the color of one's skin, or one's economic status, but a function of one's ability and desire. This goal is what access was about for my grandparents, and it is this spirit that we must continue to strive for as we attempt to build the alliance between higher education and government. Our relationships with the government must be directed to the development of policies and programs that not only preserve the great social ideal of an equal chance but make it a practical reality as well.

In considering the question, "Who decides who will be the students?" the following assumptions have been made:

(1) Access *and* choice are the dual objectives being sought.

(2) Students should be afforded real access and choice regardless of age, race, sex, economic status, or geographical location.

(3) Diversity in American higher education is not just empty rhetoric. Real choices must be available or the country's higher education system will be in danger of losing its greatest strength—diversity.

(4) In order to make access and choice a practical reality, higher education must enter into a cooperative alliance with the government.

Any list of the people or factors involved in deciding who will be the students is bound to grow rather lengthy. In no particular order, here is my list. First are the students—their parents; peers; high school counselors, teachers, or coaches; age, sex, or race; their socioeconomic status; their academic performance or special talents; their personal motivation and aspirations; their scores on aptitude tests.

Next are the institutions—their cost, size, selectivity, location, and, in many cases, religious affiliation. Other factors are the availability of financial aid and the possibility of scholarships; court decisions; affirmative action (special admission) programs; professional societies and associations; state laws; articulation agreements; faculty admission committees; availability of accurate information; academic or vocational program attractiveness.

No doubt another list would include other factors in deciding who the students will be. Fortunately, a number of studies have been done in this area, and while it is not my purpose here to present all of them, it should be helpful to review some of the major findings.

Barriers persist

(1) Whereas a college education was once determined by the ability to pay tuition and other costs, it is now popularly believed to be determined by the student's ability to do the academic work. Despite some real progress that has been made toward this goal, socioeconomic barriers persist to a noticeable extent in American higher education. One of the most sobering findings of most studies in this area is that the occupation of the student's father has more to do with college attendance than does the ability of the student.[1] Stated bluntly, even in 1978, after 20 years of massive federal and state efforts in student financial assistance, the major influence on a young person's decision to go to college is family income.[2]

(2) A student's college decisions (that is, *whether* to go and *where* to go) can usually be predicted from his or her personal characteristics. Using such information as socioeconomic background, high school record, and college plans and aspirations (but not using any information about institutional characteristics such as pricing or student financial aid), 85 percent of the college decisions made by high school seniors can be predicted with accuracy.[3] In other words, decision-making models that attempt to account for the impact of financial aid, institutional characteristics, selectivity, and costs are models which account for a mere 15 percent of all college enrollment decisions.

(3) Usually, about 80 percent of bright high school graduates (from the top two-fifths of graduating classes) with high socioeconomic backgrounds attend college, while only about 20–30 percent of the lower socioeconomic group of the *same ability level* enter college. However, the presence of a community college more than doubles the chance of enrollment for this second group.[4] Perhaps not surprising is the finding that, regardless of ability level, students travel farther to attend private

1. K. Patricia Cross, "Beyond Ability," in *The Research Reporter* (Berkeley: Center for Research and Development in Higher Education, 1967), p. 1.

2. T. M. Corwin and Laura Kent, eds., *Tuition and Student Aid: Their Relation to College Enrollment Decisions* (Washington: American Council on Education, 1978), p. 62.

3. George Weathersby, "Determinants of College Decisions," in *Tuition and Student Aid: Their Relation to College Enrollment Decisions*, p. 3.

4. Cross, "Beyond Ability," p. 4.

institutions than to attend public institutions. The lower-level ability students are much less likely to travel very far from home to go to college.[5]

The effect of financial aid

(4) How does financial aid affect the student's choice among several institutions? While more study is needed on this difficult question, the following findings seem to be consistent among most studies: (a) financial aid has a much greater effect on the probability of attendance among low-income than among high-income students; (b) tuition has no discernible effect on the high-income person's probability of attendance, but it has a significant negative effect on the low-income person's probability of attendance;[6] (c) being awarded a grant has a much more significant impact on college decisions than does the amount of the award itself, within a range of $200 to $1,200. Thus, eligibility patterns for grant assistance may be more important than the magnitude of funding; (d) there is almost no evidence to support the belief that a person accepted at both a relatively high-cost and a lower-cost college will always choose the lower-cost institution;[7] (e) when compared with grants and work-study programs, loans may act as a negative incentive, and, in fact, may discourage a student from entering college; (f) the costs of attending various institutions seem to influence students differently depending on their ability levels: students in the lower two-fifths of ability levels are more likely to enroll in a college with lower costs, while the upper level ability students do not seem as affected by price differentials;[8] and (g) college choice reflects a lot more than cost, although evidence exists that financial aid is probably an efficient way of increasing access and choice in higher education.[9] It appears that the main impact of financial aid is upon the lower-income student, and that it is the granting of the award itself, not the amount, that has the largest impact upon college attendance.

5. James Henson, "The Effects of Federal Aid on College Decisions," in *Tuition and Student Aid,* p. 20.

6. George F. Nolfi, "Supply and Demand in Postsecondary Education," in *Tuition and Student Aid,* p. 29.

7. Weathersby, "Determinants of College Decisions," p. 4.

8. Henson, "The Effects of Federal Aid," p. 23.

9. Nolfi, "Supply and Demand," p. 29.

Insufficient information

(5) There is some disturbing evidence that high school students are woefully misinformed about college costs and financial aid. A 1975 Iowa study revealed that high school seniors thought that costs were 55 percent lower than financial aid officers at the same institutions said they were.[10] Another study showed that many high school students downgraded their college plans because they thought they could not afford to attend the type of institution they preferred.[11] Virtually every study of high school students reveals that they feel they do not have adequate information about college costs and about financial aid. The situation is not altogether different for their parents, and thus access and choice are probably being rather severely limited by insufficient and incorrect information.

(6) Despite widely held beliefs to the contrary, most students apply only to a single institution. The dominant pattern is for the individual to apply to one institution, to be accepted by that institution, and to attend that institution. Thus, as George Weathersby has said,

> When we talk about the effect of pricing on student decisions, we are talking about a choice that is made very early, when people first decide to apply, not very late, when they must decide upon multiple acceptances.[12]

Unfortunately, in terms of the access and choice objective, this early decision to apply to only one institution is often based upon very limited, and often inaccurate, information.

(7) It is difficult to argue the case for subsidizing the college education of children from families with above-average incomes because the cost of education has not risen faster than these families' incomes. Despite the 45 percent increase in students' education costs between 1969 and 1970 and 1975 and 1976, the percentage of full-time students attending private institutions has changed little during this period.[13] While there is clearly a "tuition gap" between public and

10. *A Survey of Plans for Education and Careers: A View of What the Iowa High School Senior Class of 1975 Plans To Do Following Graduation and Why* (New York: College Entrance Examination Board, 1975).

11. J. S. Davis and W. D. Van Dusen, "A Survey of Student Values and Choices" (New York: College Entrance Examination Board, 1975).

12. Weathersby, "Determinants of College Decisions," pp. 3–4.

13. Joseph Froomkin, "Middle Income Students and the Cost of Education," *Educational Record,* Summer 1978, pp. 254–67.

private colleges, there is little evidence that this gap has increased during the past seven or eight years. Between 1969 and 1975, full-time enrollment increased in all parts of the public sector, but especially the two-year colleges, whereas in the private sector, enrollment declined in the nonselective institutions, remained constant in the moderately selective institutions, and increased substantially in the highly selective institutions.[14] Thus, in considering the access and choice question, efforts should be made to differentiate among institutions by selectivity. Financial aid programs have not yet had a very substantial impact on these patterns.

The myth of equal access

(8) When reviewing the success with access and choice in higher education, it must be remembered that open admissions has been largely limited to the community colleges. As Astin's research has indicated, there the student's chances of completing a degree program are relatively poor when compared with their peers who enter a more traditional four-year institution. Astin claims equal access in public higher education is a myth, because most of the weakest students attend institutions with the most limited educational opportunities, and high-ability students usually gain access to the most selective colleges, which also are likely to have the most extensive educational opportunities.[15]

(9) Despite the rather discouraging nature of many of these findings, there is reason to be hopeful and perhaps even optimistic. When provided with sufficient information and parental and school encouragement, Brookover has shown that students' aspirations for college can be significantly raised.[16] Furthermore, it is clear that a well-timed offer of financial aid, when packaged effectively, can be a positive influence on a student's decision to attend college. While college costs do not seem to be the dominant factor in college decisions, financial aid can contribute in important ways to the access and choice problem. Effective high school counseling, better and more complete information from

14. Henson, "The Effects of Federal Aid," p. 14.
15. A. W. Astin, *The Myth of Equal Access in Public Higher Education* (Atlanta: Southern Education Foundation, 1976).
16. W. R. Brookover, J. LePere, D. Hamachek, S. Thomas, and E. Erickson, *Improving Academic Achievement through Students' Self-Concept Enhancement,* Cooperative Research Project #1636 (Washington: U.S. Office of Education, 1963).

the colleges themselves, and a less confusing application process may contribute to more successful use of financial aid programs.

In efforts to make significant access and choice a practical reality, financial aid remains a factor. Christopher Jencks has said,

> While lack of money is by no means the most serious problem confronting children from the lower strata seeking education . . . it is the most commonly discussed, the most easily analyzed, and the most readily eliminated.[17]

But even with the government's massive efforts in financial aid, the answer to the question today, "Who decides who will be the students?" is still largely social class, family income, and parental expectation. Too many students are either baffled by the college application-financial aid process or make decisions based on extremely limited or inaccurate information. Such a complex problem is not easily overcome, but the Better Information for Student Choice project sponsored by FIPSE is an example of a program that offers some encouragement. Providing better information to students is critical in achieving access and choice, and neither institutions nor the government can achieve this goal alone. An alliance founded on cooperation is needed, rather than additional mandatory disclosure language in future legislation. While many people do not like the term *student consumer,* institutions must provide accurate and better-timed information about costs and academic programs if financial aid programs are to serve the goal of access and choice.

There is a great need to form an effective alliance with the government so that education policies and programs are developed that support educational goals. Astin's research on this matter indicates that too many education policies conflict with the findings of education research and have been instituted for economic, rather than educational, reasons.[18] Public systems have greatly expanded and institutions have been urged to grow larger to provide better economies of scale, despite rather convincing evidence that smaller, private institutions seem to foster greater personal growth among students. Single-sex colleges have increasingly become coeducational despite studies that consistently have shown a pattern of effects on students in single-sex colleges that are

17. Christopher Jencks, "Social Stratification and Higher Education," in *Financing Higher Education: Alternatives for the Federal Government,* ed. M. D. Orwig (Iowa City: American College Testing Program, 1971), p. 88.

18. A. W. Astin, "On the Failures of Educational Policy," *Change,* September 1977, pp. 40–43.

almost uniformly positive. Community colleges, while serving diverse purposes, have not served the needs of the traditional undergraduate very well as measured by persistence toward graduation with a bacca-laureate degree, but their lower costs have been very attractive to policy makers. In developing financial aid legislation, policy makers have been very attracted by loans, while grants and work-study programs have been shown to be much more effective in enabling students to complete college. Thus, policies and programs that are developed to improve access and choice must go far beyond economic factors, to include— in fact to be based upon—education goals and outcomes and human statistics.

A tuition advance fund

In late August, the United States Senate passed a revised college tuition tax-credit bill and the middle-income student aid bill within a twenty-four hour period. Such behavior only serves to reinforce one of the major problems identified by the Student Financial Assistance Study Group, which in 1977 stated,

> the Federal Government has no overall philosophy of financial assist-ance to students on which to build a comprehensive and logical pro-gram of support. . . . Legislation has provided a patchwork of assist-ance to meet particular problems and concerns.[19]

Surely there is a better way for such a rich nation as ours to address the critically important social goal of access and choice than simply to tack on a few more amendments to the already crazy-quilt pattern of federal student aid programs. Bold new proposals, such as President Silber's Tuition Advance Fund, deserve careful consideration, but the main task must be to establish a sensible, coherent philosophy of finan-cial assistance that serves the goal of access and choice.[20]

The current situation is not only confusing, but it is also unsuccessful in meeting the important educational need we have in this country for diversity. Furthermore, no one's interests are well served when public and private institutions are essentially pitted against one another by federal policies.

19. U.S. Department of Health, Education, and Welfare, *Report to the Secretary: Recommendations for Improved Management of the Federal Student Aid Programs* (Washington: Government Printing Office, 1977), p. 21.
20. John R. Silber, "The Tuition Dilemma: A New Way to Pay the Bills," *The Atlantic,* July 1978, pp. 31–36.

Who decides who will be the students? The answer to that question should be the student, based solely on the student's ability and desire. Having and using that option was a large part of the dream that brought my grandfather here in 1899, and that dream became a reality for his family. It is that dream which must be preserved in a new alliance between higher education and government.

American Federalism and Autonomy

STEVEN MULLER

WHO decides who will be the students? What a very American question that is! In most other nations, the question is scarcely worth asking, because there it is so clearly the national government that makes the major decisions. Throughout most of the world, government establishes and funds institutions of postsecondary education, sets out the criteria establishing who is eligible to be supported by government as a student, and controls the school system that has so much to do with the ability of prospective students to qualify as eligible for higher education. Government does not distribute native talent among children, and often does not wholly control the social circumstances that influence how such talent develops in childhood. Short of that, however, it is essentially government that decides who the students in higher education will be.

The United States is different. Only if we understand how and why the American system of higher education differs from most others; and if we examine the logical consequences of the root assumptions of our own system; only then, I believe, can we fully realize the context of the questions we ask, and the possible answers. To illustrate quickly, Americans are concerned with student choice. This concern assumes a freedom of choice that does not usually exist, for example, for a German unless he or she was earlier admitted to a gymnasium, nor for someone in the United Kingdom unless he or she earlier has passed an A-level examination. It also assumes the significance of a choice that scarcely exists, for example, in the German Federal Republic, in which in theory all universities are designed to be alike, so that the selection of one over another is largely a matter of geographic convenience.

Here, I will argue only two conclusions. One is that in the United States it is now the federal government that plays an ever increasing role in deciding who is eligible to be a student in higher education— and that this new and still burgeoning federal role is a radical but logical development within our system. The second is that the individual institution of higher education still plays a principal role in selecting its own students, and that this institutional role is traditional and logical and should continue within our system. My purpose, then, is to justify these two conclusions by rooting them in the fundamentals of the unique American system of higher education.

Higher education in the United States differs from other nations primarily because of the nature of American federalism and because of the unique mix and variety of institutions. Except for the service academies, there are no federal institutions of higher education. States, counties, and localities sponsor colleges and universities, as does the private sector. At least four major categories of both public and private institutions have developed: the two-year community or junior college; the four-year college; the university that offers both undergraduate and graduate/professional education; and the major research university. This mix and variety of institutions did not develop as the result of a plan, but has instead resulted from decisions by state or local governments or private groups to found colleges or universities that would meet expanded needs and desires for higher education. While nowadays the pace has slackened, new institutions are in fact still being founded.

A system of options

Three fundamentals of this evolving system merit special emphasis. First, a public school system developed throughout the country that does not mandate the division of students into one stream headed for higher education, and another headed elsewhere. College preparatory courses exist, but as an option. Except for their actual individual grades and talents, and except for only minor variations in curriculum, secondary school graduates are therefore essentially alike, at least insofar as all could be considered eligible for some measure of postsecondary education. It is easier to communicate my essential point here by contrast to foreign practice: American colleges and universities were not created to cater to a finite minority of students preselected by the school system. They could be and were created and expanded to draw on as much of the total pool of secondary school graduates as they chose to attract. The most highly talented eligibles among secondary school graduates, thus, were attracted by and to the most prestigious colleges and universities, but increasing numbers of other eligibles were attracted by and to other institutions. Ideally, at least, varied scales of talents and institutions met and matched each other.

Second, each institution of higher education was not only free to, but found it necessary to, orient itself to a particular segment or segments of the huge total pool of eligibles. The very diversity of talents and institutions within the whole effectively have ruled out the possibility of any one institution serving all possible needs and talents in sight. Occasional efforts by state universities to offer all things to all students rapidly resulted in so large a demand that multicampus universities were established—within which each particular campus rapidly acquired a character and clientele of its own. It is true that certain institutions have over time advanced in the scales both of quality and size, but at any moment in their evolution they remained of necessity selective, on one hand in their offerings, on the other in their students. In the early period of American higher education, privately founded colleges and universities were substantially in the majority and, over time, their basic patterns of governance and operation became the model for all later development. As a result, state and locally sponsored colleges and universities possess in the United States substantial autonomy from government, in contrast to their counterparts abroad. Typically, such public colleges and universities in this country are not operated directly under state or local legislatures, nor by state and local education departments. Instead, they function under the jurisdiction of governing boards modeled on the trustees of private institutions. They administer their own budgets, within comprehensive appropriations. Generally, they select their own students, although frequently within comprehensive guidelines, set by government, that tend to favor local residents and may mandate certain criteria of eligibility.

The concept of campus

The third relevant fundamental of our higher education system is that the size of the American college or university is limited. Several factors account for this limiting: the peculiar and distinctive character of undergraduate education that has evolved; the relative affluence of American society; and the resemblance among institutions (which is a product of their competition for their share of what has been an open market). These factors have not only given us the unique concept of the campus, which is usually residential. They have also created accepted norms of operation that affect the use of classrooms, class size, faculty teaching loads, faculty-student ratios, etc. As a result, American institutions of higher education regard themselves, and are publicly regarded, as limited in size—at least to the extent that it is taken for granted that significant increases in students must be accompanied by matching expansion of faculty, physical plant, and other supporting elements. An explosion of student numbers of the kind that has taken place in Italy, for example, or in some Latin American countries—without matching expansion in other respects—would fail in the United States because it would be perceived as inappropriate and inadequate. A consequence of this fundamental, then, is that American colleges and universities enjoy the privilege of limiting their own student numbers, which buttresses their right to select applicants to fill the available places.

We have been witnessing in recent years a mounting effort by the federal government to create increased parity of both student access and choice to colleges and universities. This trend follows a more egalitarian interpretation of the Constitution, the passage of new and deliberate egalitarian legislation, and public demand. It has involved all three branches of government. Its principal concerns have been to eliminate arbitrary exclusion of students based on race, sex, and physical handicap, and to remove lack of economic means as an obstacle to the opportunity for higher education. It is not necessary here to cite the particulars. It is sufficient to recognize that the equalizing of access has become a federal, rather than a state, responsibility; that the federal government in creating the basic opportunity grants has assumed a vast new role, compatible with what national governments do abroad but radically innovative in American experience; and that the federal government has been willing to use its fiscal power to compel higher education institutions directly to abandon discrimination based on race, sex, or physical handicap. We should note also that in general the federal government has done little to help create new institutions of higher education, except for occasional measures, such as the health manpower leglislation, specifically designed to foster the expansion of institutions in selected critical professional areas. In essence, the federal government has been working with the existing, still evolving mix and variety of institutions.

A crucial borderline

Now we arrive at a crucial borderline between the new role of the federal government and the traditional role of the institutions of higher education in deciding who shall be the students. The new federal role appears logical in the context of the American system of higher education insofar as its purpose is to strengthen the pool of eligible applicants. This purpose is achieved when discriminatory exclusion is outlawed; when economic resources are made available to applicants; and even when special benefits support a special group of applicants, such as veterans. But while the federal government, thus, has much to say about eligibility, its purpose in this respect does not automatically extend so far as to direct all or any one institution to accept a particular applicant or a particular class of applicants. The federal government, in other words, can and will play a major role in deciding how the pool of potential students will be composed, but the government will not assign students to institutions.

Such a distinction is sensitive because of the way in which the concept of academic freedom has evolved in the United States. While elsewhere in the world, the idea of academic freedom has expanded little beyond the commitment to freedom of teaching and learning stated by Wilhelm von Humboldt in the early nineteenth century, the idea in America has come to embrace the larger notion of institutional autonomy for college and university. The right of an institution to decide on the size of enrollment and to select its own students is perceived to be as much a part of institutional autonomy as the right of the college or university to select its faculty, establish the curriculum, and administer its funds. All these rights are encompassed within the understanding of institutional academic freedom in the United States. This reality is again best understood by contrast, i.e., with the recognition that American professors in government-sponsored colleges and universities are not civil servants; that government does not mandate curricula; and that public as well as private institutions of higher education manage their own budgets internally. The American concept of academic freedom includes the idea that political power shall not exploit the education process or institutions of higher education. Therefore, an attempt by the federal government to assign students, and to remove the right of student selection from colleges and universities, would be perceived as a direct assault on the academic freedom of American higher education.

Competition for fewer students

It may strike some people as amusing to speak of institutional selection of students at a time when colleges and universities appear to be competing for students from what is at present a pool of declining size. Also it is obvious that the methods of providing assistance to students which the federal government employs may have a great impact on the ability of types of colleges and universities to attract students, as independent institutions, for example, have been persistent in pointing out. Nevertheless, little reflection is needed to confirm the significance of the border between the federal government's role of enhancing eligibility and the institutional role of selecting students. Even colleges and universities competing for undergraduates will still wish to employ criteria of recruitment and acceptance. Evidence for that can be found in the resistance to federally imposed quotas to implement affirmative action, as demonstrated even by institutions willing to impose quotas voluntarily upon themselves. Incidentally, it should be noted that open admissions does not necessarily violate the principle of institutional selection of students, as long as it is an option exercised by decision of the institution and not imposed by government. In the American setting, where students are graded for each successive course rather than only once in a comprehensive examination when they complete an entire curriculum, open admissions in any case more resembles selection deferred to a later stage than a commitment to allow any person, regardless of ability, to complete the curriculum successfully.

With respect to graduate and professional schools, there are still too few places generally for too many eligibles. In actual fact, the intention of the federal government to assign specific students to specific institutions and the resistance of universities to this intention arose last year as a result of health manpower legislation. A section of that legislation called for the secretary of the U.S. Department of Health, Education, and Welfare under certain conditions to assign certain kinds of students to medical schools receiving a particular type of federal support. Leading universities and their medical schools refused to accept support on this condition, and Congress then amended the condition out of the legislation. The claim of the universities, to which my institution and I were party, was that the assignment of specified students by the federal government violated institutional academic freedom.

Of course, the decision to be a student in higher education remains at its very heart a personal one on the part of each person, influenced by a web of circumstances that surrounds personal talent and ambition. On the one hand, however, the federal government has assumed the responsibility for assuring that individuals shall not be denied access and choice to higher education on the basis of race, sex, handicap, or extreme economic deprivation. On the other hand, each individual college and university retains the right—within the law—to define its size and to decide who shall be admitted to be its students. As long as we retain the mix and variety of colleges and universities that has evolved, the assignment of students to institutions by the federal government would, for the individual, abrogate free opportunity rather than enhance it. For the institutions, it would violate academic freedom as presently defined and practiced.

Students and the Admissions Decision

ALFRED L. MOYÉ

ONE OF the most important questions to contemporary man is who should go to college and who should not. Educators, legislators, philanthropists, economists, sociologists, lawyers, civil rights activists, and even deputy commissioners spend a great deal of their time talking about this important social question. Fortunately, we have not reached an "eternal" consensus, but rather our opinions, requirements, and suggestions form a confluence of factors that influences the eventual outcome of admitting a particular student to a particular school.

The importance of this process cannot be underestimated, and can be demonstrated by the point that not being admitted to a college is similar to not getting into heaven—there is no comfort in numbers.

For this reason I have chosen to focus on the primacy of the student in the process, and approach the subject from his or her viewpoint—who and what determines if and where I shall go to school? To this end, I will briefly describe what I see as the most important internal and external forces contributing to an admission decision. Then, given my particular vantage, I would like to discuss in greater detail one specific external force—the federal government—and its involvement in the process of matching students to schools.

Currently, over eleven million students are attending 3,100 colleges and universities. Literally hundreds of thousands of other persons are engaged in some form of postsecondary education in a variety of schools, institutes, and training centers of business and industry. Students are full- and part-time. They are young and old. They come from every walk of life imaginable and they all have different dreams and aspirations of what personal gains are to be realized as a result of their investment of time and money. The really interesting matter to ponder, though, is how the match between all of these students and all of these forms of postsecondary education comes about? I believe that the answer lies in a kaleidoscope of internal (students and institutions) and external (governmental, professional, and organizational) forces that merge to shape the aggregate match.

In a democratic society, one which prides itself on the freedom exercised by its institutions, a system of higher education has evolved which is diverse and which, on the whole, has the capacity to serve all those seeking its benefits. Students are relatively free to select the institutions most suited to their needs.

The primary forces affecting who determines who goes to college is the interaction between schools and prospective students. From the institution's viewpoint, the admissions officer is the person accountable for carrying out the policies of the institution. Some institutions have well-defined policies and the task is less difficult. Others have poorly defined goals and the job becomes more arduous. Policies range from totally open admissions to a very select, meritocratic system of applicant acceptance.

Without government intervention

In their admissions practices, institutions variously take into account prior scholastic achievement, test scores, special abilities (peer group leadership, athletic abilities), special personal characteristics, and potential contributions to a profession. Institutions often choose to build academic and social communities through their admissions policies. Because students learn from each other, these communities are themselves educational mechanisms. The institution, without government intervention, has the right to interpret or create its own public policy without undue interference, without loss of academic standards, and without loss of institutional autonomy. The key participants, of course, are the trustees, the academic administrators, the faculties, and in some instances, the student body. To the extent that they collectively participate in and clearly fulfill their obligations, the smoother the process works; the applicant pool can be reduced to those individuals who can benefit from the type and quality of education offered at that institution.

This construct leads to the second half of the primary equation—the prospective student. I believe that the student still is the principal participant in the admissions process. No one else is responsible for what a student's transcript looks like but the student himself. No one else can determine a student's extracurricular activities and leadership potential but a student, and no one takes the standardized admissions tests but the student himself.

Naturally, the students are influenced by their parents, by their counselors, and by their peers in selecting those institutions to which they will seek admission. The larger question for many, however, is whether or not it is going to be beneficial at all in reaching personal goals, or when will be the right time to "drop in." Fortunately, in our system these questions of when, why, what, and where regarding a college education are still principally questions that in the first instance must be answered by the individual.

The secondary forces

College attendance is not totally a matter of concern between institutions and students. Other forces are at work. All of the beneficiaries of higher education and all of the entities that support the higher education enterprise have, to varying degrees, a say in who decides who will go to college.

- Organized labor has an interest.
- The professions are very much involved in determining who will be trained to enter their ranks.
- Donors and philanthropic organizations help to shape college admissions policies.

- The church for many institutions and individuals has always played a major role in determining who within their sector goes to college.
- Business and industry have a distinct stake in the quantity and quality of trained manpower.
- Public and private elementary and secondary schools influence in many ways the nature of our postsecondary education system—certainly as a user of the trained manpower pool but, perhaps more importantly, as the provider of the education normally prerequisite to the college education.
- State and local governments are definitely an external force as they carry out their public welfare responsibilities.
- And then there is the federal government—perhaps the most powerful external influence and, for many people, the influence that causes higher educators the greatest concern.

The relationship between higher education and the nation's welfare became a critical subject for public discussion during the 1960s. There was heightened recognition that higher education had a formative influence on the men and women who most affect our social, political, and economic development. College and university education was viewed as the principal means of achieving upward social and economic mobility. Given this consensus on the importance of higher education as a social institution, federal policy makers focused on how the federal role could complement state and institutional goals most effectively. The admissions process was identified as a major link between social justice and education goals.

Federal encouragement

The federal concern has been articulated by law, by executive order, and through regulation. All three branches of government have participated in encouraging higher education institutions to swing open their doors wide to people of all ages aspiring to postsecondary educational opportunities.

The Congress as far back as 1862 with the passage of the Morrill Act has influenced decisions on who goes to college. Then, the concern was for more people trained in the arts of agriculture and mechanics.

After World War II, the challenge was to open college education to returning veterans. The GI Bill and the College Housing Act both made dramatic changes in college enrollment patterns.

In 1958, the National Defense Education Act influenced the higher education enterprise to rethink and reshape enrollments in science, mathematics, engineering, and foreign languages.

In 1963, the Congress found that

> this and future generations of American youth be assured ample opportunity for the fullest development of their intellectual capacities, and that this opportunity will be jeopardized unless the Nation's colleges and universities are encouraged and assisted in their efforts to accommodate rapidly growing numbers of youth who aspire to a higher education.

The result was the passage of the Higher Education Facilities Act of 1963, which provided the incentive for colleges and universities to expand their capacities to enroll more students.

In 1965, the Congress further expanded the federal role by initiating a program of grants to low-income students; a new guaranteed loan program to supplement the direct loans provided for in the 1958 act; a program addressed to the community service and continuing education needs of the country; and the authorization of project grants to "developing" institutions. All of these measures have had profound effects on college enrollment.

That same year, 1965, the health professions education assistance amendments provided scholarships for students in the medical professions as well as institutional support to improve the quality of medical education.

A broadening of roles

In the 1967, 1968, 1972, and 1976 amendments to higher education legislation, there has been a steady broadening of these basic roles. The emphases on student aid and on the broader concepts of postsecondary training opportunities have characterized the Congress's intentions in these subsequent enactments.

The Congress has influenced college enrollment in other, perhaps less subtle, ways.

• In 1964, with the passage of the Civil Rights Act, it stated that institutions receiving federal assistance shall not discriminate on the basis of race, color or national origin.
• In 1972, it prescribed that no person on the basis of sex shall be excluded from participation in any program or activity receiving federal assistance.
• In 1974, Section 504 of the Rehabilitation Act of 1973 made similar provisions for the physically handicapped.

My purpose in citing these facts is to underscore that yes, the Congress, through passage of social legislation, has in fact altered the ways colleges and universities enroll and educate students.

If I were asked to predict future policy changes, I would guess it would be in the area of studies for part-time (less than half-time) adult learners. Our current tax policies and our current student aid policies are not doing a whole lot to encourage adults—people now in the labor force or retired persons—to benefit from the kinds of new opportunities available to them in our nation's higher education institutions.

The courts have made their impact on admissions felt in *De Funis, Bakke, Adams,* and countless other decisions. In *De Funis,* particularly in Mr. Justice Douglas's opinion, affirmative action took on new meaning. He suggested ways and means for institutions to broaden student selection criteria that would not be discriminatory, but would rather improve upon traditional methods of admitting students.

In *Adams,* litigation which has been in the courts almost a decade now, the single reminder is that in states where discrimination was by law a way of the past, these states must now act affirmatively to collect racial dualism. Recruitment nets must be thrown out in such a way that applicant pools provide institutions with individuals from racial groups that they historically have not served.

Bakke and affirmative action

The Supreme Court ruling in *Bakke* sanctions the affirmative action activities of many institutions across the nation, including activities approved and supervised by the U.S. Department of Health, Education, and Welfare.

The Court ruled that when institutions have illegally discriminated against individuals from minority or disadvantaged groups, those institutions can be required, under the Constitution, by the government to adopt and carry out affirmative action programs.

These rulings strongly support this nation's continuing effort to live up to its historic promise: to bring minorities and other disadvantaged groups into the mainstream of American society through admissions policies that recognize the importance of diverse, integrated educational institutions.

These rulings also provide support for HEW efforts under Title VI of the Civil Rights Act of 1964 to end illegal discrimination in education through affirmative action programs. The principle of affirmative action has been constitutionally reaffirmed.

More carrot than stick

The executive branch of government has made its impact also on college participation. HEW in particular has shouldered most of the burden for administering the education laws of the 1960s and 1970s which fostered institutional reform insofar as college participation is concerned. The department has also been instrumental in enforcing the civil rights legislation that affects schools and colleges. If I were to generally characterize the department's efforts, however, I would say they are "mostly carrot and leastly stick."

The guiding principles of this administration (and for previous administrations) have been that:

1. Federal dollars for postsecondary education are best directed at providing opportunities for the disadvantaged.

2. Most of the money should go to students, rather than to institutions.

3. *Access* to higher education is best achieved by attempting to eliminate financial barriers to college attendance.

4. Student's *choices* of institution or educational program should be the deciding factors, rather than price.

5. There are sufficient capacity and sufficient resources available for everyone with the desire and ability to go somewhere—to enroll full-time or part-time—in a program that meets their needs.

6. Retention or chances of completion of an academic program should be maximized through federally funded but institutionally directed remediation and counseling services.

7. Institutions which are now or which have historically served large numbers of economically, educationally, and culturally disadvantaged persons require added resources to improve the quality of their curriculum, faculty, administration, and student services.

OE and student choice

The Office of Education's student aid programs have probably had the greatest effect on the institutional student profiles regarding federal goals of access and choice, with the result that greater numbers of students have gained new freedom in selecting colleges and academic programs.

Today, as a result of federally supported programs, many more different kinds of people are attending college than previously—racial minorities, the physically handicapped, low-income students, educationally deficient students, persons with socially or culturally different backgrounds, older students, and women.

In the bureau I head, almost all of the twenty some programs we administer carry with them an implication for shaping college enrollment patterns. Programs such as Upward Bound, Talent Search, Special Services, Educational Opportunity Centers, Educational Information Centers, Teacher Centers, Cooperative Education, Continuing Education, Strengthening Developing Colleges, the Graduate and Professional Opportunities Program, CLEO, the international programs, and others all carry with them an opportunity for the recipients of such support to mold a new response to who goes to college.

From my personal perspective as a recent university administrator and now a federal executive, I have witnessed a very positive and creative partnership in the making between the federal government and the higher education community. I think it is because the social policies that have been passed into law over the past two decades are, in spirit, consistent with the social commitments of educational policy makers. I believe also that the new partnership has been due to the government's greater willingness to use the carrot rather than the stick in advancing these policies. Perhaps most of all, the partnership has flourished because we have had the good sense to let students have primacy in deciding who will be the students.

5

Who Decides About Research?

Federal Support
for Research

LINDA S. WILSON

AN INTERPLAY of external and internal stimuli, resources, and restraints determines what research is undertaken in institutions of higher education. The stimuli include, for example, individual investigators' ideas and interests, various needs and desires in society, and opportunities arising from matching questions with capabilities for answering them. The resources include the knowledge base, adequately trained personnel, facilities, and funds. The restraints include various external legal and political interventions as well as internal plans and priorities.

The balance of external and internal forces in the interplay among research stimuli, resources, and restraints shifts from time to time. The potential for shifts in this balance has kept attention focused for more than thirty years on the basic problems of assuring institutional integrity and freedom for scientific inquiry, or, in other words, on the challenge of assuring appropriate opportunities for institutional and individual choices.

Influence of federal funds and restraints

The subsidy of academic research by the federal government has been a matter of particular interest. Sponsored research evolved from a fractional part of higher education's responsibilities in the 1930s into a major campus activity for some institutions in the 1970s, and it produced a major expansion of the scientific capacity of the nation. The opportunities provided by federal research sponsorship have been very attractive: accelerated scientific progress through research; strengthening of institutions' capacities for research and advanced training; and incentives for individuals to undertake graduate study.

Certain dangers have also been perceived, however, in the expanded federal involvement in research and higher education. Sixteen years ago the Brookings Institution published a report on the effects of federal programs on higher education[1] (including research support programs) and identified the following dangers of federal support: domination of national interests over the fundamental pursuit of knowledge; suppression of unpopular ideas; growth of bureaucracy and consequent modification of the nature of the academic institution; political dictation of what should be taught and who should teach.

Perhaps it would be useful to assess the extent to which two of these threats have been realized. Consider first the effect of federal research sponsorship on academic investigators' research choices.

The processes by which funds for research are allocated involve extensively the scientific community, including academic scientists. Scientists participate in identifying national research objectives, in setting priorities among them, and in developing strategies for achieving them. How do these choices affect individual investigators?

In 1976 the American Council on Education reported[2] the results of a survey of doctorate-level departments in sixteen selected science and engineering fields on the extent of faculty involvement in research; the number of faculty with external research support; the extent to which such external support was primarily for research outside the faculty member's preferred area; and the factors influencing faculty to select externally sponsored research outside their preferred areas. The

1. Harold Orlans, *The Effects of Federal Programs on Higher Education* (Washington, D.C.: The Brookings Institution, 1962).
2. Frank J. Atelsek and Irene L. Gomberg, *Faculty Research: Level of Activity and Choice of Area* (Washington: American Council on Education, 1976).

survey revealed that more than four-fifths of the full-time doctorate faculty spent at least 20 percent of their time on research; that three-fifths of those spending at least 20 percent of their time in research had external support for it; that only 10 percent of all externally supported investigators were being supported outside their preferred areas, and most of these were working within their field but in a different subfield or specialty within their preferred field; and three-fifths of those working outside their preferred area did so because they believed they could find better opportunities for support there.

The report showed some differences among the sixteen disciplines surveyed. In economics, mathematics, psychology, and sociology, a majority of faculty members who spent at least 20 percent of their time on research did not have external support. Furthermore, a greater percentage of faculty in economics, electrical engineering, sociology, and botany worked outside their preferred areas. The data for faculty in departments ranked by a study by Kenneth Roose and Charles Andersen[3] as "distinguished and strong" indicated these faculty members spent more time in research; more of them had external research support; and fewer had external support for research outside their preferred area. Even among these stronger departments, however, some fields (in particular, botany and economics) had less congruence between support and faculty preference. While the survey data indicate that the research interests of faculty members in institutions offering doctoral programs do generally coincide with the availability of external support and choices, it is clear that external funding is influencing significantly what research individual investigators undertake.

Next, consider the effect of federal research sponsorship on the academic institutions. The substantial federal subsidy of research has affected institutions' choices and the process of making those choices. In the period when federal research support expanded rapidly, the government encouraged institutions to strengthen their capacities in specific areas of national interest. Institutions derived considerable advantage from this process, but they also had the difficult task of maintaining overall balance among fields with major disparities in the resources available for this purpose. A decision not to accept federal funding for

3. Kenneth D. Roose and Charles J. Andersen, *A Rating of Graduate Programs* (Washington: American Council on Education, 1970).

a specific project or for development of a specific area could be a decision to accept the loss of key faculty members, who sooner or later would move to institutions where federal support would be available. Recent examples of the federal emphasis on the development of research centers and institutes and institutional response to that demonstrate the vulnerability of the university to the pressure of the federal dollar. The National Science Foundation's program to develop a theoretical physics institute and the National Institutes of Health's program to develop national centers for cancer and other catastrophic diseases forced institutions to choose between pursuit of an objective about which many had grave reservations or probable loss of some key faculty.

For institutions that emphasize research productivity in tenure and promotion decisions, the influence of federal choices in the funding of research areas can also affect indirectly the composition of the institution's faculty, especially in those fields in which research is quite costly.

The process of applying for, distributing, and accounting for federal research support has necessitated the development of an institutional bureaucracy to cope with these functions. Because the federal requirements frequently differ from the institution's own requirements, the institutions receiving federal support have had to change in more ways than simply expanding to accommodate a larger research function. In some cases the federally imposed management standards fit poorly with fundamental aspects of the institution. A key example of this poor fit has been the imposition of detailed monthly time and effort reporting for multimission activities. As one might expect, when federal and institutional standards diverge, the institutions' accountability is questioned, and public confidence in institutions diminishes. The result can be increased specificity of requirements and decreased public support for scientific research. Both results ultimately affect research choices.

Federal regulation of research introduces additional restraints on research choices. The increasing specificity of federal regulations in recent years has amplified their impact on academic institutions. For example, in 1962 approximately one-third of the academic departments of medicine required committee review of the use of human subjects in research. Most institutions had indiosyncratic methods of review and documentation, but their objectives were the same. Not long thereafter, the federal government imposed committee review as a requirement. Today the bureaucracy created by this federal requirement has grown substantially and is expanding still further. Overregulation of research discourages research that is likely to require unnecessarily complex review or control, and it escalates both the financial and the human cost of the review and monitoring process. Few would argue against protecting human subjects. The question is whether all the bureaucracy imposed is really necessary for the purpose. In this area as in others, the problem of appropriate assessment of the risks and benefits of research as well as the costs and benefits of prior review of research needs to be addressed and balanced against the cost of research forgone.

Distribution of responsibilities

The decision-making processes that finally result in research choices involve the participation of Congress, federal agency leaders and program managers, the Office of Management and Budget, various advisory councils, consultants, and the public, including institutions, scientists, and laymen. Given the complexity of the decision-making process, how can academic institutions make proper provision for institutional autonomy, avoiding or minimizing dangers such as those mentioned?

Academic institutions must commit resources for research that are consistent with their commitment to research. Insufficient commitment of resources provides no basis for implementing internal choices and makes the institution vulnerable to external pressures.

Academic institutions must take quite seriously the responsibility to review proposals submitted for research support, to review the terms and conditions of agreements resulting from them, and to review the basic management standards and procedures imposed by the research projects.

The research project system of support offers multiple, discrete, and recurring opportunities for institutions to exercise choice. Institutions have a responsibility to decline support that results in unacceptable intrusions on institutional prerogatives. The process by which new management requirements are imposed also includes opportunity for institutions to review and comment. Institutions must resist constructively the imposition of unproductive management requirements.

Academic institutions have a responsibility to consider the effect of their individual choices on the nature, role, and functioning of the university as an entity in society. The opportunism or irresponsibility of individual institutions can undermine the independent and apolitical character of the university, which is vital to a free society.

Academic institutions must regulate themselves if they wish to avoid external interference. They must address squarely the issues of ethics, good management, and quality of performance. Yet these issues must be approached in ways consistent with the nature of the institution and its governance. While the ultimate responsibility in some of these matters must lie with researchers, the institutions must assure that the institutional environment both stimulates and rewards individual responsibility.

Given the government's extensive participation in the decisions on what research is undertaken, what special responsibilities accrue to it?

It is essential that those persons involved in making and implementing government policy and procedure truly recognize the particular role and function of universities in our society. They must also understand the nature of the institution, including its necessary differences from other organizations. Universities bear the responsibility for articulating these matters, but their responsibility must be matched by a government commitment to recognize and accommodate the nature of the universities so that policies and procedures can be appropriate and effective.

The government must consider the long-term implications of its research support policies and procedures in order to assure research capacity. The research project system provides excellent opportunities to choose what research is to be supported, but makes no provision for sustaining the capacity for research. Universities alone cannot provide adequately for this need. The burden must be shared for the long term national interest.

The government has a responsibility to keep the regulatory process under control so that any regulations that affect research do not stifle the essential creative process or impose unnecessary burdens or costs.

The overall system by which research choices are made in this country has been generally productive and satisfactory. Universities have played an important role in meeting the nation's scientific needs. But the relationship between universities and the federal government has become troubled, primarily because of a divergence in their expectations. Prompt resolution of these differences will be essential to avoid deterioration of a relationship important to both the government and the universities.

Factors in Research Funding

FRANK PRESS

NO INDIVIDUAL or institution alone is qualified to determine what research a society's scientists should do. The mix of research is determined by a number of factors. One important factor is the current state of a specific discipline (for example, the intellectual curiosity it has developed). Another factor is the expectation it has created of its future support and the value of its possible results. An example of the former is black holes, of the latter, genetic engineering.

Government supports different types of research for different reasons: because they are projects of high developmental cost (space); because their payoff is distant (fusion); because they are big science, requiring very costly equipment and facilities (high energy physics, oceanography, astronomy); because they are of high social or economic value (cancer, energy).

Some fields of research are funded favorably because they are ripe; that is, there is a consensus that the research is close to achieving a breakthrough or opening up new areas of knowledge in a specific field. Some ripe areas today are biological nitrogen fixation, solar-terrestrial coupling, neurochemistry, submicron structures, laser chemistry, tropical biology.

Public pressures also influence the direction of research support. Nuclear waste management is one example of this. The environmental and consumer movements were historic in their influence.

The pros and cons of a more rational system are often argued. The dangers of overregulation are cited, and the omniscience of any groups in society to determine or control scientific research is doubted. We must make some judgments concerning perceived needs, but it is just as important to create the climate and conditions to allow science and the scientist to flourish freely in a society that respects and supports the pursuit of new knowledge and its beneficial application for humanity.

Science and Government

CORNELIUS J. PINGS

LET US consider: Who should decide what research we do? How are people chosen to do the research? Do the same people and processes make the decisions for pure and applied research? Does the system of making decisions work in the best interest of science? Of scientists? Of the universities? Of society? If not, what are the difficulties and what might be done about them?

Who should decide?

The reflex answer of a scientist to the question of who should decide what research is done is, of course, the scientist. Perhaps a more realistic answer is the scientific community. Although the scientific community does control much knowledge, it has little in financial resources. In current times relatively few scientists are independently wealthy at a level that would support meaningful laboratory research, and there are very few free-lance patrons of the sciences. Most worthwhile research in the natural sciences today requires substantial facilities and supporting budgets for equipment and personnel. Most scientists, therefore, are employed and supported by a variety of agencies. The sources of funds include the universities and colleges, the states, the federal government, industry, and private foundations—the modern equivalents of the court patrons of earlier centuries.

It is a fundamental premise that the donor of funds will decide how and for what the money is to be spent. But the principle is in conflict with the practice in the case of scientific research. Every king and president may be accepted also as a general or admiral, but few would assert themselves in the role of chief scientist. The message is clear; patrons of science can only make wise decisions on allocations of required wealth by seeking the advice of the scientific community to establish priorities and measures of quality. It is obvious, however, that such a situation creates a potential conflict of interest, and the scientist would be well advised to note that message. In California, Proposition 9, passed in 1972, has created a circumstance in which any individual knowledgeable about an issue is automatically disqualified from participating in or influencing public decisions.

Fortunately, on major scientific issues a willingness to accept the wisdom of the scientific community in guiding national science policy persists. Committees of Congress generally listen appreciatively to testimony from scientists; the executive agencies are largely dependent on external boards, advisory panels, and individual reviewers; foundations usually have advisory bodies and/or depend on a peer review process; university administrators fortunately still come largely from the ranks of scholars and defer to faculty advice. Even in large-scale scientific endeavors the use of special facilities is largely controlled by an appropriate scientific community. How much money to spend on accelerators, telescopes, and other one-of-a-kind installations is clearly determined by decisions in the Office of Management and Budget and in congressional committees. These decisions are also guided by advice from the scientific community. The underlying reasons for some very large programs or facilities often relate to national security or national scientific preeminence, and political forces often enter candidly into the selection of sites for such projects. But the scientific management of the facility is usually vested in acknowledged scientists or science administrators; telescope time or time on the beam is determined by people who actually use the equipment, active investigators in the field, who vouch for the scientific integrity of the experiments carried out.

A possible conclusion is that the scientific community is one of the few remaining enclaves of society that significantly controls its own destiny, even though others provide the wherewithal. If such is the case, the arrangement is tenuous and is based more on tradition than on any absolute right.

Who does the research?

Standard wisdom is that the best science is done by the best scientists, by and large in the best institutions. But the system is elastic and accommodating. The outrageous idea may still emerge; the lesser institution occasionally nurtures an outstanding young research scientist or engineer. The brash young investigator, however, usually learns to play the game—float enough new ideas to titillate the peer review panels, but do not get caught in unnecessary controversy. Meanwhile, the dean and department chairman of an emerging institution know full well the reward and the penalty of nurturing extraordinary promising scientists; the euphoria that follows the first recognition of their work is usually followed by offers from the establishment universities. No wonder congressmen rail at the apparent "Massachusetts-Colorado-California axis" in science funding; no wonder higher education sometimes finds it difficult to speak with one voice on matters of public policy; no wonder women and minorities indict the entire system for apparently denying access to the top ranks of university research careers.

Where is the system defective? Perhaps in always attempting to work in the best interests of science, which may not always be in the best interests of the currently emerging generation of scientists. A case might be made that the scientific community is too scientific about the business of science. It knows really quite well how to establish mechanisms to make reasonable assessments about proposed scientific work or to judge the results when work is submitted for publication. That strength in the system has enabled scientists basically to determine how funds should be directed by willing public and private donors. The same system does not do so well, however, in judging potential scientists.

Pure and applied research

If research is really applied, the sponsor should usually be involved in setting the plan of research and in monitoring progress. The sponsor's involvement includes the prerogative to deny the investigator the right to pursue interesting developments that are not apparently germane to the stated objectives of the investigation. Such work, therefore, has a dubious place on the campus and is particularly inappropriate for graduate thesis work.

Of course, these comments are not meant to apply to associated laboratories or large mission-oriented projects. The major research universities have a proper role in serving the national interest through special laboratories or programs committed to defense, space, energy, or other major national problems. In such cases the university community certainly assumes responsibility for assuring competent management and the highest standards of science and engineering in the work carried out. In the very large operations a small portion of the budget may be deliberately set aside for basic research; such work should be carried out with appropriate scientific independence. But the fundamental mission of such laboratories must be significantly directed and monitored by the funding agency. The university in turn needs to be vigilant to avoid intertwining faculty, students, support personnel, and facilities in any manner that would restrict the openness of the research environment on the main campus.

Does the system work?

By and large the university campuses support an amazingly effective basic research enterprise. The principal external sponsor, the federal government, seems generally pleased with the results, although there are occasional expressions of concern about geographic concentration of funds or about the legitimacy of some of the research projects. Most of the carping about projects is from a very few congressmen seeking publicity. The majority of congressmen and their staffs understand the relationship between university and government and support it with sound appropriations. The current administration is particularly supportive of the role of basic research in a highly technological society.

Science research and education are doing well on the campuses. Certainly, grant and contract funds are not now at the level they were in the 1960s and early 1970s, but those years were the anomalies, and there should have been no rational expectation that research funding would indefinitely increase at rates of 8 to 15 percent a year.[1] As that era resulted in a larger and healthier university research enterprise, the universities have had to face adjustments to budgets that have shown relatively little real growth and, under the previous administration, even some erosion. Although the administration of Jimmy Carter fought this year for increased funds for research, the effort was undermined by fiscal caution in Congress. Nevertheless, even though funds are tight, there are relatively few complaints that the good university scientists are unfunded or critically limited in their programs. Furthermore, after several years of stagnation in faculty staffing, universities have generally resumed hiring assistant professors, and in some disciplines quality candidates may even be in short supply.

Recent years have shown some improvement in federal funding for the social sciences and the humanities. Funding for the humanities is particularly significant because higher education in the United States has entered an era of enrollment decreases that could raise havoc with the arts and humanities programs, which are the very core of the universities.

Let us acknowledge that there are problems and deficiencies. A common campus complaint is that research equipment is obsolete. Research in the physical sciences and engineering seems ever more expensive, usually leading the national inflation. Science by its nature is progres-

1. Daniel J. Kevles, *The Physicists* (New York: Alfred A. Knopf, 1978).

sive; with last year's equipment one can usually do little more than repeat last year's experiment, occasionally to profit, but usually not. Most funding agencies recognize the need for continual infusion of more sophisticated apparatus, but often the Office of Management and Budget and Congress are more conservative in approving funds. In order to cope with the heavy financial burden of high-technology experimentation, the universities on their part are probably going to have to show more initiative in developing arrangements for sharing expensive facilities, both on the campus and regionally. They have already accepted this trend for the large physics and astronomy experiments; the National Science Foundation is currently experimenting with regional facilities in chemistry. Every investigator would like a private laboratory, but maximum use of the limited funds available for equipment suggests that it will be expedient to share the equipment and hence the funds. This will have implications beyond mere inconvenience; as faculty and graduate students travel to the equipment and do their experiments, there will surely be some disruptions of both faculty and graduate student ranks. In the extreme, deans and department chairmen may be presiding over departments that are at any given time largely on detached duty, a situation that would have serious implications for teaching continuity and campus commitments. In the meantime, one hopes that Congress and the executive agencies can withstand pork barrel temptations in locating such regional facilities.

The universities also face serious problems of stagnation deriving from the lack of growth or even atrophy of faculty ranks. Some scientific areas may appear to have at least temporary shortages of candidates, but most disciplines face a long period in which they will be able to hire very few new Ph.D.'s. How can the universities maintain intellectual stimulation? How can they avoid the disastrous situation of essentially excluding several academic generations from faculty ranks? There is no single answer, and the educational community needs to work more avidly on early retirement programs, more active leave and exchange arrangements, enlarged postdoctoral or intern programs, and so forth. The academic community must expect to solve its own problems, but this matter should also merit help from the public sector on the grounds that otherwise this nation's research capability will be seriously eroded.

The relationship between the federal government and the universities has also spawned some outright antagonisms. One hopes that they are intrinsically petty, but even if so they seem persistent and increasing. For example, there is almost constant questioning of the adequacy and fairness of the peer review system. University business officers and their government counterparts are engaged in seemingly never-ending debate over cost accounting principles; during the last year and a half one could start a predictable diatribe in any university business office by simply muttering, "A-21." Government auditors and financial officers seem in many instances to feel that universities and colleges are managed in mysterious and therefore probably unacceptable ways. An ever encroaching set of strictures forces the universities toward conformity and uniformity. The government feels that there must be a higher level of accountability for public funds. It would be unusual if there were not some merit to both points of view. Unfortunately, the ongoing dialogue has at times generated more rancor than wisdom.

During the last eight years or so a new area of strain has developed between the universities and the federal government. This area encompasses the group of laws and regulations including affirmative action and all of its manifestations, Title IX, Internal Revenue Service regulations on racial discrimination, recent regulations on access for the handicapped, and others. In most instances the universities must respond to these regulations because they accept federal funds for research. Is it not ironic that the academic community has more freedom in the pursuit of the research than in the administration of assorted social action programs? Surely institutions of higher education can be counted on to perform better in research than as agents of social change. After all, one of the strengths that the university community offers is a thread of stability and continuity in a society that is buffeted by political, economic, and social pressures. That very stability negates rapid accommodations to new mandates on staffing faculties and changing the composition of student bodies. Funds are always short on most campuses, and some academics cling to the idea that the available resources should be directed to education and scholarship rather than to ramps, locker rooms, and an ever increasing administrative structure.

The federal government has asked—indeed demanded—that the academic community lead on matters for which it has little experience and no resources. Those groups that feel they have been denied access surely have a right to expect fulfillment of reasonable expectations; the universities might never have responded to the challenge without some goading, but highhandedness of style and failure to provide the necessary funds by the federal intermediary have caused resentments that will likely be longstanding and may compromise future cooperative ventures. Science and scholarships are healthy in the United States, and much credit is due the public sector, which has supplied substantial research funds but has generally not interfered with the direction of research. Some new problems may arise as scientists adjust to national and regional facilities for the more expensive programs. Meanwhile, the existing modes of support should not be taken for granted. The university community should be prepared to define sharply and defend the need for ongoing fundamental research in this country and must simultaneously be vigilant to protect the integrity of such mechanisms as the peer review system, which are central to self-control.

There are some problems. Scientific research occasionally falls out of favor with an administration or a congressional committee, often because the universities have failed to communicate the importance to the society of a stable, independent, campus-based research enterprise. There are too many strains over administrative matters, and too much of a limited resource is squandered on squabbles and negotiations between the business agents and lawyers. We have a sound system, but many agree that something has gone wrong in the basic relationship, and if uncorrected the situation is likely to worsen. Perhaps it is time for a national commission to inquire into the university-federal relationship involving the funding of research.

6

Who Decides What to Spend?

Federal Involvement in Spending

ROBERT M. ROSENZWEIG

IN ONE way or another virtually everyone is involved in deciding where higher education spends its money. University trustees and administrations are involved in obvious ways; faculties are involved through the direction of their intellectual interests and personal needs; students are involved through their curricular and career preferences, and frequently through their political and ideological preferences as well; staff members are involved through their unions or through the operation of the marketplace; local, state, and federal governments are involved through appropriations, mandated activities, and various inducements; and the general public is involved as the parents of students, electors of legislators, and alumni of institutions.

Nevertheless, there are clearly different degrees of responsibility among all those parties, and the important and interesting questions are how the responsibility for fiscal decision making for institutions of higher learning is distributed and whether the balance is shifting over time.

The question of where higher education spends its money is not, at bottom, one of finances. Rather, it is a question of power and its distribution, of autonomy and its value, of high social purposes and their conflict. For all of these money is a surrogate, a convenient symbol for summarizing a cluster of issues that have to do with the constraints under which colleges and universities must operate.

There are not very many generalizations that can be put forward with confidence about higher education in the United States. One that seems to have some merit, however, is that those institutions of higher learning, public and private, that are generally considered the best have a relatively high degree of independence from their principal patrons. In other words they are better able than most institutions to determine their ends and their means free from direction and control by legislatures, wealthy donors, and other external forces. But the important part of that description is the word relatively. There is no such thing in this world as a wholly free agent, and because these are very important social institutions, it would be quite undesirable for them to be beyond the reach of outside influence.

With that important qualification, two points can be inferred from the generalization. First, there is some kind of relationship between independence from external direction and academic quality; and second, since the institutions in question are generally those of highest reputation, the society as a whole recognizes the importance of independence in institutional decision making, or at the very least values the results of independence.

There is good reason to believe that the latitude for independent decision making that colleges and universities have enjoyed is being eroded and that the main instrument of that change is government.

Curiously, in spite of all that has been said and written in recent years about the baneful effects of government intervention in education, it is not easy to define with precision just what this diminution of institutional autonomy amounts to. The universities complain about this or that set of regulations and about increasing paperwork and costs; they are experiencing difficulties over hiring practices, confidentiality of files, access to files, and literally dozens of other specifics. The areas of relatively independent decision making are being narrowed. But it is difficult to give it all shape, to assess its meaning, and to understand its consequences.

It is very difficult to come to grips with this condition because it is a condition that no one intended to produce. If institutions of higher education were the victims of a conspiracy, or of an ideology, or even of a coherent set of policies, they could, perhaps, understand their source and their purposes and begin to deal with them. But none of those is in fact the case. Instead, those institutions are the victims of the least glamorous and most characteristic affliction of modern social policy—the unintended consequence.

This affliction is particularly acute in connection with those actions of the government that are not directed at institutions of higher learning as educational institutions, as institutions doing business in an increasingly regulated economy. The list of areas with which the government concerns itself has grown very substantially in recent years and includes, but is not limited to, labor law, social security, retirement, safety, privacy, and the employment aspects of civil rights legislation. This class of government activity has been the source of large direct and indirect expense, growing bureaucracy within institutions, a great deal of litigation, and an enormous amount of controversy. Taken together, these repercussions of government involvement have significantly limited institutional freedom of action, and the structure of the political system generates very little incentive for the advocates of particular measures to care about that result. That assertion warrants explanation, because it lies at the core of the present condition.

The political system of the United States was quite consciously designed to make it difficult for government to act. The arrangements for separate centers of power and elaborate checking devices that characterize the federal government provide an abundance of opportunities to veto an action before the final, presidential veto need even be contemplated. Therefore, in order to have a chance of success, a public policy idea must have a constituency, an organized, effective, vocal constituency. Furthermore, in many of the matters that concern higher education, the issues are frequently cast not as public policy choices but as moral imperatives.

The policy-making process, then, tends to consist of organized and articulate groups pressing for the redress of a perceived injustice. Their force, both political and moral, frequently overwhelms such complications as questions of timing, cost, the ability of institutions to respond to new demands, and the relationship between means and ends—between the problem perceived and the remedy proposed. All such questions tend to be seen merely as excuses for delay, as arguments by the rich and powerful to protect their wealth and power. No one has stated that position more clearly than Governor Jerry Brown of California who, when signing into law a measure that eliminated any mandatory retirement age, said that among the many letters he had received on the issue, supporters tended to be individuals, while opponents "tended to be from the universities, corporations and other holders of power. This is a classic case of gigantic institutions putting their own archaic work rules ahead of individual freedom."

The debate over mandatory retirement recently completed in Congress is an instructive example of the problems that concern higher education. The legislation was pressed by a potent interest group, and it was certainly not aimed at colleges and universities in particular. When it became clear that legislation was likely to pass, there had still been virtually no consideration of how a change in retirement age might affect educational institutions whose "work rules," if not archaic, are certainly unusual. When educators finally awoke to what was about to happen, they mounted a last minute effort, which not even the most charitable observer could describe as the careful or reasoned analysis that the subject demands.

One might argue that educators had no real case, that faculty members are entitled to work under the same protections as everyone else, that colleges and universities are not different from any other employer. Any or all of those arguments may be correct. What is beyond dispute, however, is that in enacting a national retirement age of seventy years Congress removed from institutions of higher education a part of their ability to decide for themselves the most desirable age distribution for their faculties, an area of policy that has critical consequences for teaching, research, affirmative action, and the future of the academic profession. That Congress could have moved so far toward a major change in social policy without consideration of, or perhaps even knowledge of, its effects on a set of institutions on which the society relies so heavily, suggests, at the very least, a lack of balance in the deliberative processes.

It should be understood that this case is only an example. The point that it illustrates—the profound effect on institutions of higher learning of governmental actions to which they are barely a party—is general and is repeated in many other areas of policy.

If the independence of these valuable institutions is important to their quality, then somehow that important value needs to be weighed explicitly against the claims put forward on behalf of other important social values. The argument that justice delayed is justice not done must be met by and balanced against the argument that the cause of justice and of the institutions that must be the instruments of justice can be undone by the excessively single-minded pursuit of particular purposes.

Since it is unlikely that the U.S. political system will change fundamentally, and since in any case it is difficult to imagine another that would serve better, there can be only one remedy to the imbalance that has crept into the system. The independence of institutions of higher learning will be protected from further erosion only to the degree that those who are responsible for those institutions are alert and aggressive in protecting their interests in the legislative process.

The difficulties of that course of action must not be minimized. Not the least of them is that, on occasion, those who speak for higher education will find themselves on the unpopular side of particular issues, and even at times at odds with their own students and faculties. But the plain fact is that no one will speak for the long-range interests of institutions if those to whose care they are entrusted are not willing to do so.

State Support for Higher Education

JAMES M. FURMAN

VIRTUALLY every institution of higher education in the United States is involved with state government, and many, not all of them public institutions, are utterly dependent on continued state support. No one needs to be reminded of the fundamental importance of state government to higher education.

The importance of higher education within the total framework of state government is equally obvious. The states have made a tremendous investment in facilities and in the human resources of colleges and universities. Every year the states allocate from 10 to 25 percent of their revenues to support higher education. The states' investment in higher education is compelling evidence of a genuine belief in higher education's social value.

It is difficult to imagine any truly fundamental change in the relationship between higher education and the states; the current relationship is an uneasy one and may be even more uneasy in the immediate future.

This paper will first describe some of the important forces that affect the relationship between the states and higher education and then suggest some ways that the parties to this alliance might reduce the dissonance in the relationship.

State governments and institutions of higher education have a common objective: to make the benefits of education and scholarship available to the people. This common goal cannot be overemphasized, but it would be naive to ignore differences in institutional and governmental perspectives as they seek to achieve this objective.

Higher education administrators and faculty members will naturally seek to maximize the resources they have available to do their work. The surest way to be considered a successful college president is to increase faculty salaries, find support for additional positions, and maintain stable or slightly increasing enrollments. It is difficult to imagine an academic community seeking a leader to reduce costs and eliminate staff positions.

The natural institutional drive to maximize resources inevitably collides with an equally natural governmental objective to minimize taxes and expenditures. It is equally difficult to imagine a political campaign in which a candidate emphasizes his commitment to increase taxes, and recent events make the prospects for such a campaign even more remote. The pressures on elected officials to hold the line or cut back on taxes must be very similar to the pressures on college presidents to obtain more resources for their institutions.

When taken to an extreme, either institutional efforts to increase revenue or governmental efforts to control taxes can work against the ultimate objective of providing necessary educational services. Institutions may find themselves establishing programs of questionable value or lowering their academic standards to maintain or increase enrollments. The ultimate effect of such strategies is to tarnish the credibility of valuable, cost-effective programs within higher education. On the other side of the coin, the governmental pursuit of controlling expenses can lead to penny-wise, pound-foolish strategies that impair the quality of higher education.

Autonomy is another area of significant difference between institutional and governmental perspectives. The literature of higher education is filled with eloquent and persuasive defenses of academic freedom and administrative autonomy for colleges and universities. While there are occasional exceptions, government and higher education seem to have established a working consensus on the principles and operation of academic freedom. The question of administrative autonomy, however, is more troublesome. Clearly a substantial degree of administrative flexibility is essential to the effective operation of higher education. But there is a fine line between the degree of flexibility required for effectiveness and the degree of flexibility desired for the convenience of administrators. Quite naturally all administrators seek to increase their options; it is important, however, to recognize the legitimacy of certain governmental forces that limit that flexibility.

Political leaders feel the need to maintain control and accountability over publicly funded services as intensely as they feel the need to minimize taxes. As a practical matter elected officials have been inclined to grant substantial operating autonomy to the administrative leadership of colleges and universities. But they believe strongly that they are ultimately accountable for the use of public dollars. The rhetoric of educators who desire institutional autonomy is often in direct conflict with the rhetoric of public officials who are accountable to the electorate.

The difference between institutional and governmental perspectives on the issue of autonomy sometimes appears in subtle ways. If the seminar in which this paper was first read had been planned by some elected officials, the title would not have been, "Who decides what to spend?" It would have been, "Who decides where higher education spends the taxpayers' money?"

While elected officials can be persuaded to give administrators a useful and appropriate amount of flexibility, they have a legitimate and understandable need to maintain control over publicly supported activities. Admittedly, efforts to maintain control and establish accountability sometimes lead to overregulation, excessive data collection, and unproductive conflict, but the right and responsibility of elected officials to control the use of public expenditures is apparent. The usefulness and effectiveness of various means of ensuring accountability need to be reexamined.

Most of us can remember when the primary concern of state government was to provide enough resources to expand higher education services. The governmental objectives of minimizing taxes and maintaining control and accountability existed, but they did not receive the emphasis they receive today.

Higher education is entering a period when few outside the education community see any need to expand higher education. Even the optimists within higher education tend to think that existing enrollments can be maintained, not that they will grow. Those within state government who have other priorities are looking forward almost eagerly to the prospect of enrollment decreases.

Everyone knows that the goals of minimizing taxes and maintaining control and accountability are very much in the minds of governors and legislators and the staff of the legislative and executive branches. There seems to be a growing awareness of the negative aspects of regulations at the federal level but little of that sensitivity at the state level. Instead, the number and sophistication of the professional staff serving state legislators and governors is growing rapidly. The time-honored need for skills in personal and political relationships is still very important, but more people are involved in the process, and their questions are tougher to answer. Hard analysis and good data are becoming more and more essential to establishing trust and justifying requests.

There are a number of ways higher education can improve its relationships with state government. Government officials expect higher education to advocate greater support for its programs, but they also appreciate sensitivity to and acceptance of their role and of the countervailing pressures with which they deal. Sometimes as government officials exercise their role of skeptical critic, defensiveness in higher education hinders communication and damages credibility. Such defensiveness can suggest that unfavorable information is being withheld, or it can insult the intelligence or question the values of a critic, who may be uninformed, but is neither stupid nor harmless. Sometimes defensiveness can turn a discussion into a duel, which from the perspective of higher education makes about as much sense as a cocker spaniel challenging a tiger.

All this is not to say that higher education must or should be passive in the political process. Higher education needs constantly to remind itself and government that they share the primary objective of providing high quality educational services. Discussions over the means to that end can be meaningful if they emphasize the mutual goal.

The best way for higher education to avoid defensiveness in such discussions is to anticipate criticism and take the initiative to solve problems. This requires a high level of self-awareness within higher education (a strong argument for good management information systems) and a responsiveness to questions that demonstrates openly that problems are recognized and dealt with. In short, the best way for higher education to improve its relationship with government is to be obviously well-managed, responsive, and cost-effective without giving the impression of arrogance or conceit.

On the other side of this relationship, state governments must avoid a heavy-handed pursuit of efficiency and accountability that impairs educational effectiveness. The states need to ensure that different perspectives on secondary objectives do not keep higher education and government from achieving the common objective of providing quality services to the public. The states need to listen carefully to higher education and to ask the tough questions that naturally come in the political process.

The state coordinating board can be a useful mechanism for maintaining productive dialogue between government and higher education. When first established, state coordinating boards were often seen as policemen whose job it was to regulate competition and dampen the aspirations of expanding public universities. While that role still exists to some extent, state coordinating agencies can also make a major contribution to state higher education relationships as a third party with a combination of both perspectives. A state coordinating agency finds it easier than institutional administrators to be constructively critical of higher education because it is not as dependent on the support of the university constituencies. At the same time, the state coordinating agency is not constantly compelled to worry about the political danger of a tax increase or the demands of other government supported services. It is also less likely to become involved in partisan maneuvering, even though its proximity to the political process may make it more sympathetic to and understanding of the forces influencing elected officials.

While the state coordinating agency cannot and should not merely pass on institutional perspectives to state government, it can and should develop an appreciation and understanding of complexities of higher education. This kind of expertise will give higher education the benefits of a sympathetic ear within government and will give government the benefits of an impartial, informed view of higher education needs.

In short, the role of the coordinating board ought to be that of subtle advocate for higher education during the coming decade. This role requires:

1. an unqualified commitment to and appreciation of higher education's mission
2. the critical examination of higher education for ways to improve services and achieve the governmental goals of accountability and cost-effectiveness
3. a careful and creative search for ways to achieve common objectives through cooperation and discussion, not through bureaucratic regulation.

As subtle advocate the coordinating board can add the weight of objective opinion to the case for higher education's needs and provide an arena for thoughtful discussion and mutual problem solving as government and higher education seek the common goal of high quality, cost-effective educational programs.

Finally, let me emphasize that the extent to which state coordinating agencies can be effective depends largely upon the willingness of both higher education and government to use them in this role. No state agency has enough power in and of itself to establish effective relationships between higher education and state governments. But the coordinating agency can make a major contribution toward effective relationships if government and higher education take full advantage of its strengths. It is in the best interests of both to do so.

7

Who Champions the Institution?

The President Speaks
for the University

JOSÉ A. CABRANES

TO SOME extent the question "Who champions colleges and universities?" may be recast as the question "Who is entitled to speak for colleges and universities?" In other words, who acts on behalf of the institution in confronting the demands or claims upon the institution asserted by the community beyond the academy?

In most nonacademic organizations the chief executive officer is the principal outside contact—the person to whom the world at large looks for authoritative statements of the policies and preferences of the organization. The representative functions of a chief executive officer of such organizations are recognized and tolerated by the external community because it is invariably assumed that the chief executive officer is more than merely a spokesman for the organization. Indeed, the representative functions of a chief executive officer are enhanced by the generally accurate assumption that the chief executive also exercises effective final authority in the internal affairs of the organization—that the chief executive is, within well-understood limits, the organization's unquestioned boss. In business organizations, labor unions, and other nonacademic organizations, the effectiveness of a chief executive officer in external affairs is diminished to the extent that that person's authority in internal affairs is openly disputed.

These observations on the politics of organizations have some important implications for academic institutions, however different they may be from one another. Yale University, for example, is organized somewhat differently than the general model of university governance that I would like to address. It is an unabashedly traditional institution whose administration is, in my view, relatively uncomplicated. Its presidency is a strong presidency, as suggested by the fact that the president is not only a member of the governing board—the Yale Corporation—but also its presiding officer. But even at the older universities in the United States, it is fair to say that no single officer or group of persons governs in a way comparable to the chief executive of a nonacademic organization.

Educators speak of "collegial governance" and frequently of the institutional "community" when they speak of decision making in a university. Committees shaping university policies are often constituted to be clearly "representative of the university community," which is one way of assuring that their recommendations will be acceptable to the various constituencies that by implication have some role in the governance of the institution.

Although we like to think of higher education as different from other social and economic enterprises, the theme of the annual meeting at which this paper was first read (Higher Education and Government: An Uneasy Alliance) reminds us that higher education is increasingly regarded by the state as just another regulated industry.

The application to higher education of regulatory schemes originally designed for other corporate structures is sometimes disturbing. These schemes are disturbing, in part, because the hierarchical presumptions that govern corporate behavior are not precisely replicated in colleges and universities. Government may prescribe a rule, but a university president may not readily have the means to apply the rule within the university. The governance of institutions of higher education, as a federal appeals court recently noted, is "unique and has no counterpart in the commercial business models" that some statutes are designed to regulate.[1]

1. National Labor Relations Board v. Yeshiva University, Docket No. 77-4182, Slip Opinion, p. 29 (United States Court of Appeals, 2d Cir., July 31, 1978).

Despite some grumbling to the contrary, in most institutions of higher learning the tenured faculty members remain the most important group of decision makers in the community, because they are the group within the organization with the principal long-term or permanent stake in the future of the place. The decision of the U.S. Court of Appeals in the case of *Yeshiva University*[2] reminded us that the full-time faculty of traditionally organized institutions have managerial status—that is, they are not simply employees of the institution.

In recent years students have successfully claimed significant roles in the governance of institutions of higher education, including participation in major policy committees, in search committees for ranking administrators (including presidents), and even on the governing boards of institutions. In some colleges and universities alumni and nonfaculty staff members have claimed an important role in governance.

A simple reality lies beyond the felicitous and significant references to collegial governance, the university community, and the partnership of diverse university constituencies; in a university no single person is clearly the boss. Although occupants of the White House occasionally turn to university presidents for major assignments as cabinet officers and high-level administrators, partially on the assumption that they have run a large organization, it remains true that university presidents are in no sense comparable to the chief executive officers of other organizations in our society. They are more closely analogous to the conductors of orchestras; a good university president brings to an agglomeration of talented and highly individualistic virtuosos a unifying conception of the relationship of all the players to the common enterprise. Like a conductor, a university president uses an understanding of the central, unifying idea of the enterprise, the experience gained through a professional background, and leadership skills to help each of the participants understand what the whole is about. If the university president is skillful and lucky, he or she will be able to project this unifying idea internally to the players and externally to observers.

But even a conductor of an orchestra presumptively has greater authority over the individualistic members of the orchestra than most university presidents have over their faculties and students. An openly rebellious or discordant orchestra member can possibly be banished; a university president rarely, if ever, has such disciplinary powers over

2. Ibid., p. 30.

faculty members. A university president is expected to reign rather than rule, to persuade rather than dictate.

The peculiarities of university organization make it difficult, though not impossible, for a university president authoritatively to champion the interests of the institution in its dealings with the external world. A president's hand will be strengthened by the high regard in which society holds higher education in general (and perhaps the institution in particular) and by the considerable status presumptions that are perquisites of the office. A president's strong personality, leadership skills, and intimate knowledge of the institution's processes can make a difference; they can overcome seemingly insuperable obstacles of organization.

But a president's authority to champion the institution in its dealings with the real world, or to keep the institution financially solvent despite the special claims of different university constituencies, is often questioned—questioned by the very constituencies with which the president shares power internally. In a period of scarcity, economic contraction, and widespread anxiety about future prospects, relationships among the various university constituencies become adversarial, and even a president's claim to spokesmanship in external affairs may be subject to dispute and overt challenge. Any university administrator who has lived through a strike of some of its staff will recall demands by some students or faculty members—who may share authority for governance—that the president yield to the demands of the striking union, because the president does not truly represent the university in the matter. A state legislator called upon to act on the budget of a public university would find it difficult to identify the authoritative spokesman of the university while being simultaneously lobbied by the groups representing faculty members, nonfaculty employees, and students, as well as by the administrator who claims to be the leader of the institution.

When universities are asked to devote their institutional resources to the solution of major social or international problems, as they have been asked to do in the past two decades, the democratic model invariably is invoked. They should resolve the issue, if they are truly democratic institutions (so the argument goes), by putting the question to a vote of the university "community." Even matters traditionally regarded as the province of the university president and the board of trustees, such as the management of the university's investments and other fiduciary functions, become subject to the demands for democratic decision making.

Because universities are now so significantly dependent on external sources of support, it was perhaps inevitable that internal university constituencies would carry their competition with the president beyond the walls of the academy. The challenge by internal constituencies to the role of the president as the champion or spokesman of the university in its external relations is nowhere more clearly demonstrated than in the proliferation of national higher education associations. Public policy for higher education is, in some measure, the product of the interaction of national associations of teachers, students, business officers, governing boards, and other internal constituencies. For many observers of this merry-go-round, organizations such as the National Association of State Universities and Land-Grant Colleges or the Association of American Universities do not champion *universities,* but rather the *presidents* of universities.

The results of this competition for authoritative spokesmanship—for the right to champion the university—cannot be underestimated. It has made it more difficult for universities to assert the basic values of institutional autonomy and self-determination in opposition to the federal regulatory intrusions that inevitably followed increased federal subventions.

All of the university's constituencies pay homage to the principle of institutional autonomy and self-determination. All invoke the blessings of academic freedom. But few hesitate to carry questions of internal governance into external arenas, asking that government agencies or legislatures render a decision different from that made within the walls of the academy. Budgetary decisions made within a state university may be challenged in the state legislature by representatives of the university's faculty or staff. Aggrieved faculty members or students, having failed to win satisfaction within the institution, turn for help to administrative agencies and the courts. In 1976, for example, some student organizations encouraged congressional efforts that would have established federal standards and federal remedial procedures for the allocation of student activity fees at colleges and universities throughout the country.

In all such cases—cases that are by no means unusual—the interests of the university are formally represented and championed by the presidents or central administrations of the institutions. The central university administration is called upon to defend the principle of university autonomy, to resist efforts to convert universities into extensions of the state, but inevitably the strength of the institution's position is eroded by the competing claims to spokesmanship that are made by important university constituencies.

All educators agree that universities should account for the efficient use of every public dollar they receive. All educators agree that public monies must be used in conformity with constitutional requirements of nondiscrimination. But some educators worry that the expenditure of public monies for particular purposes is frequently used as leverage for regulation of other, unrelated matters.

There is widespread agreement in the higher education community that universities should vigorously resist efforts to make higher education merely another regulated industry. There is a consensus that higher education ought not to be just another sector of the economy, subject to perfection in accordance with standards established by a national ministry of education. But this general agreement on broad principles more often than not breaks down in the face of the special interests of university constituencies. Under the banner of student rights, consumer protection, accountability, and other sacred shibboleths of the age, these constituencies seek the protection and support of government for their special interests.

Though properly distressed by the governmental intrusions into the academy, educators ought realistically to face a simple fact; universities may be no better organized to resist the external threats of the 1970s than they were to resist the internal threats of the 1960s.

The effectiveness of the defense of institutional autonomy is directly related to the cohesion of the university community in facing the external challenge. The symbol of this cohesion must be, in the last analysis, the university president. The vitality and autonomy of an institution of higher learning can best be defended against external threats by its president, who presumably understands and articulates the common purposes of the institution's varied constituencies and is best able to speak for the institutional community as a whole.

The academy historically is the home of independent minds. It is not, and cannot be, the sort of institution that always speaks to government with only one voice. But we should hope that a university's various constituencies will recognize the long-term damage they may inflict upon the institution—upon all institutions—by engaging or invoking governmental processes to resolve matters of internal governance. The enlightened self-interest of a university's constituencies lies in the exercise of self-restraint in external affairs and in lending support to the external relations functions of the university's president. A strong and credible president is the best possible guardian of the autonomy and freedom of the academy.

In this area, as in others, there is still some wisdom in the comment reportedly made by the founder of the University of Pennsylvania at the signing of the Declaration of Independence: "We must all hang together or most assuredly we will all hang separately."[3] If a university's constituencies can somehow manage to hang together, their president will be the voice for their common interest in academic freedom and university autonomy. If they hang together, their president will have the authority and credibility to defend the institution against policy makers whose goal is the perfection of our institutions through regulation. If they hang together, their president may be able to persuade policy makers that sometimes imperfection with freedom is preferable to perfection without freedom.

An Uneasy Alliance?

REATHA CLARK KING

WHILE government regulations at both the federal and state levels have helped to close the gap between rhetoric and reality in the mission of higher education, these regulations have also contributed to the dizzy feeling of many higher education administrators and the lack of confidence with which they make decisions. But the higher education community must be just as confusing to legislators as laws and regulations are to educators. Computers, which require an unrelenting stream of paperwork, confuse matters further and enable one group to communicate with another group. All this confusion has led to an alliance between government and higher education that gives rise to uneasiness in some, cynicism in others, and even peace of mind in other people within colleges and universities.

Let us first acknowledge that the locus of effective decision making

3. Carl Van Doren, *Benjamin Franklin* (New York: Viking, 1941), p. 551.

for management of higher education institutions has shifted from within the institution (as it used to be) to some new point in the overlapping realms of authority and responsibility between higher education and government. Each new regulation imposes a new set of constraints for decision making, to the point that educators keep searching for an optimal solution to any problem, whether it pertains to personnel practices, financial aid for students, or some other issue. For example, just as some institutions had developed reasonably good affirmative action plans, new legislation on the mandatory retirement age was passed. This forced some institutions to adjust their personnel plans, taking this additional constraint into consideration.

Let us also acknowledge that, unlike previous years, colleges and universities today have some friends, few defenders, no protectors. Perhaps the obvious protection was also lacking in the past; but the public certainly expressed more support than it does today. As public support is so uncertain, higher education is left to depend on champions from among the various constituent groups that make up the colleges and universities, perhaps among the legislators, and perhaps some from the public.

The difficulty with finding real defenders of colleges and universities relates to the fact that today's alliance between higher education and government is *not* uneasy for most of the constituency within the institutions. Many faculty and students actually trust government as the champion and protector of their interests and well-being, while they distrust the actions of their institutions. They believe that legislators pass laws and courts interpret them to protect people in higher education institutions from decisions the university might make that would adversely affect the human rights of the university's own people. An example is the impact of Title IX of the Education Amendments of 1972. While within a given institution, some administrators and faculty are complaining about the extra paperwork generated by Title IX and about its interference with local decision making, others in the same institution are happy about the law. There are numerous other examples of how government regulations are cheered by particular constituent groups within the higher education community. Thus, the champions of the institutions versus government will vary with the issue at hand.

The forums available to colleges and universities to represent their positions or points of view are the same forums that are available to the students, faculty, and other constituents who wish to contest decisions that affect them. These places include collective bargaining, law suits, arbitration, the news media, and lobbying in the legislative branch. There are no special places that offer protection for colleges and universities aside from those that bring the institutions into confrontation with their constituents. Therefore, government regulations at both the federal and state levels tend to divide the "house" of higher education and to generate an unlimited number of "family squabbles."

The problems noted above, along with numerous others, have forced on us a certain sense of humility that says it might make more sense to represent our positions humbly to government rather than to worry about being gallant champions. Perhaps the appropriate questions to address are the following:

Do we, as educators, really want strong champions of higher education institutions versus government, and what must we do to establish them?

Do we personally want to be considered champions for our institutions?

Do we wish a special arena or turf to champion from?

The answer to each of these questions is certainly yes.

The first order of business then is to stake out some turf. Higher education must get the ear of society if it wants influence with government. It must look to the broader society for stronger respect for what is going on in the institutions, and at the same time it must look to government for relief from the interference with local decision making authority and other discomforts usually attributed to overregulation. By a "broader society" I mean a variety of groups in the population, not just a select few. Many government regulations relate to affirmative action, access for people to educational services, and equal employment opportunity. If the institutions of higher education can improve their effectiveness by serving more people and by improving the quality of the services it provides to those people, then they should be able to wield more influence with government at all levels.

The American Council on Education's new office on self-regulation is a step in the right direction for relief from government regulations. If implemented, each of the planned strategies of this office should be helpful. The strategies are:

1. development of background papers and case studies intended to map out the implications of self-regulation in general and for specific situations and problems;

2. systematic efforts to identify emerging issues of self-regulation (national, statewide, regional) and to take constructive steps to offset the need for governmental regulation;
3. coordination with existing committees and projects where self-regulatory approaches have already been used or could be used more systematically;
4. communication with governmental officials (state and federal) to monitor and discuss perceived needs for regulation and to explore the extent to which the higher education community can work with government agencies to resolve problems.

It is also in order for the universities to seek relief from regulations when they are confident that they have responded to government's reasons for the particular regulation in question. If we educators can make progress with the purposes of regulation, with affirmative action, equal employment opportunity, citizen access to educational opportunity, we will get the public on our side, and can then confront government like true champions.

Because of what governmental regulations have helped institutions of higher learning accomplish for people, educators need not feel so uneasy about the higher education-government alliance. If educators look to the purpose of the regulations, respond in good faith to achieve those purposes, and then communicate forthrightly with government agencies when the administrative bureaucracy becomes unproductive, they will be the true champions for colleges and universities.

Higher Education: Its Own Champion

STEPHEN JOEL TRACHTENBERG

WHEN I was a boy, the word champion reminded me of St. George slaying a dragon on behalf of a fair maiden. My mind's eye focused on a simple conflict between easily distinguished good and evil. Today, nothing is that simple. First, dragons are now protected by militant groups of environmentalists. Both George and Perseus now work for the American Society for the Prevention of Cruelty to Animals. Second, maidens (fair or otherwise) have, in the words of the cigarette advertisement, "come a long way, baby." They can take care of themselves very nicely. Thank you all the same, but take a walk, St. George! Third, the concept of a champion presupposes that there is an agreed upon viewpoint, moral position, or even practical interest to defend against something inimical.

Those of us in the academic community may be able to agree, at least in broad principle, about the threats and the challenges from the outside, about the something inimical, about the "them." "Them" may be the federal government imposing new strictures, regulatory or fiscal, upon academic freedom of operation; or the courts ruling on the sometimes apparently opposed rights of civil liberties and academic freedom; or state legislatures determining through budgetary measures that tax-supported institutions need to practice more austerity; or corporations believing, in view, say, of Professor Smith's recently published exposé of the health hazards of the widget industry, that Everyman University is too misguided to deserve their continued patronage.

"Them" may even be those who ought to be "us"—parents who believe that young John's education is not practical enough, or that Jane's is too vocational, or that campus life-styles permit loose living; alumni who feel that good old Everyman University has changed (for the worse of course), that it is no longer a place they can comfortably regard as alma mater and, therefore, that it is no longer a place meriting their support.

What we are not so sure about is "us." (Any bridling at my blithe appropriation of the first person plural pronoun, nominative or accusative, reinforces the point.) Today's sharply defined constituencies—administrators, faculty, students, staff, and others—that together compose the contemporary college or university community make the prospect of one acceptable advocate, even for a single institution, less than realistic. When it is escalated one step, intramural disagreement becomes interinstitutional conflict. To begin with, the independent and taxpayer-supported segments of higher education are at odds. And within these sectors, disputes occur among the subdivisions. Among independent institutions, those somewhat liberated by endowment and those heavily dependent on tuition often prepare their agendas differently. Similarly, within the hierarchy of tax-supported institutions, from the large state universities with their grand medical and law schools down through the state colleges to the local community colleges and technical colleges, the institutions sometimes squabble like heirs contesting a will. And on the outside, with a point of view all their own, are the proprietary institutions of education, which can be extraordinarily persuasive with lawmakers when they demonstrate that they are small businesses that pay taxes and provide a public service, a service obviously needed, because students vote with their feet and their wallets to come. One may be forgiven for thinking of that curious, apparently purposeless head-clashing somewhat reminiscent of Brownian motion, the rugby scrum. I do not want to belabor sports metaphors—that has been done sufficiently by one of the "thems" simplistically tagged as Washington—but the spectre of an academic internecine free-for-all is alarming when only a coordinated team effort, intramural and inter-institutional, will bring higher education, not without bruises and some changes in game plan, through the problems and the challenges of the 1980s. The great twentieth century philosopher Pogo, with his sublime insight into the human animal's incredible capacity for self-sabotage, is right once again: "Them" is "us."

Nor is the problem confined to a simple myopia or malevolence on the part of a "them" out there. After all, particular human agents, whether individuals or groups, would be subject to persuasion or conquest by our champion, if there were one (and if the champion and the academic community accepted a coherent position to champion). Larger intractables confront us as well—a shrinking college-age population coupled with the spreading, and perhaps healthy, perception that not everyone needs a college diploma, rising costs resulting from inflation and the demands of expensive but necessary academic initiatives, to identify only two of the most obvious. It is sobering to keep in mind that, according to the National Association of Independent Colleges and Universities, more than 115 independent colleges have closed since 1970. Forty more have been forced to merge, and the trend will continue. Recall the words from *Ten Little Indians,* "and then there were none."

Let me descend from the philosophical sublime to the practical mundane and offer a couple of examples of the real issues that confront higher education. These are issues that we do not address in a united way, because the various constituencies, sets, and subsets identified above see them differently, because no one voice can be the champion of all academe and assume the authority to speak unequivocally on behalf of the institution *writ large*. I shall confine myself to recent events in my own backyard, the point being that no administrator of a college or university need go farther to find problems.

Example one. This spring the Connecticut General Assembly passed a bill, effective January 1, 1979, which makes illegal the retention of any specific mandatory retirement age for all personnel employed in the private sector. No special consideration was provided for institutions of higher education. Neither our unique personnel practices nor the problems created by projected declines in enrollment impressed the legislature. Even as college and university presidents sought to persuade legislators that the state law ought not exceed the provisions contained in a similar law recently enacted by Congress, lobbyists for a major faculty group argued on behalf of the language ultimately enacted. Who has gained from this new law? Who has lost? Where is right and wrong on this issue?

As the president of a large but underendowed independent institution, I am concerned that the legislation may limit faculty opportunities to recruit young colleagues and call into question under unhappy circumstances time-honored arrangements about faculty career paths. I fear that our capacity to respond to affirmative action and other similar, vital socially oriented initiatives will be reduced. Chances for promotion and tenure would seem to be diminished. Teaching and scholarship may well be deprived of the fresh ideas and vigor expected to come from junior faculty members who would normally ensure an institutional future.

Example two. A local newspaper recently carried articles about a strike of the clerical personnel at a neighboring university of prestige and wealth. The stories reported that students there were planning a benefit concert to support the striking workers. In another article the newspaper reported that the faculty also sided with the striking workers; indeed, short of a negotiated settlement, they favored binding arbitration. (What will be their position, one wonders, concerning outside mediation in some possible future dispute between faculty and administration?)

Who then seeks to frustrate the clerks and why? I know the president of the university. He is a gracious, thoughtful person with a commitment to what universities are about and a humanistic and compassionate posture toward those who compose his campus community. Is this civilized man the university? If so, why is he behaving in a manner so contrary to his nature? What obscure animus does he hold against clerks? Why, in the face of demands from students and faculty alike, does the president (or is it the university? or is it "they"?) continue to resist? Does the president perhaps think that in denying the clerks what they wish, he is somehow serving the university? If he is, then presumably he is serving the faculty and the students. Why do they misperceive what he perceives? Why does he see their interests differently than they do? As Yul Brynner says in *The King and I,* "It's a puzzlement."

Perhaps the problem, at least in the instance I use above, has to do with different notions about the availability and extent of resources. The president perceives the limits of those resources; faculty and students see their boundlessness. An endowment in the millions can seem like a lot of money until an administrator has to figure out how to stretch the income dollars to respond not only to the clerks, but also to the faculty, the electric company, the oil company, and the rest. Is the matter then one of communication? If all the students and faculty members had the same body of information that is available to the president, would unanimity reign? Are the questions, the priorities, the choices so obvious that, with all the relevant data in hand, they answer themselves? Would faculty members and students have time for anything else if they were inundated with all of the information that comes to the president's desk? Who champions the university? And for what? Against what?

No one is so naive as to believe there are not legitimate crosspurposes and conflicting interests among the various constituents of higher education. Our common purposes and mutual interests must override our differences, however. The college and university community is faced with personal austerity and challenge, which can only be met by candid and constructive dialogue on campuses and among campuses. Certainly, there is more to unite us in the academic community than to divide us, if we see our case clearly.

The philosopher Alistair MacIntyre has observed that one of the awful conditions of life in modern times is that people tend not to have goals beyond the scope of their personal appetite and desires. Perhaps it is because the distance and the divergence between proximate and ultimate self-interest usually seem great enough to ignore the ultimate self-interest with impunity. But we do so at peril to more than ethics.

Under the pressures of unplanned growth and accelerating change in almost all areas of contemporary life, the dimensions and play space of the ecosystem Buckminster Fuller calls "this spaceship earth" are diminishing in all their interlocking systems—natural, individual, institutional. The interconnections are becoming closer, more inexorable if not clearer. Sooner or later, short-sighted self-interest must hurt even the interested self.

It is a time for academic sovereignty and resolve, a time for the academic community to champion itself, but this can come only from the united will and judgments of all its constituent parts. No single voice can or should determine, articulate, and apply the priorities necessary in this situation. The resiliency and character to save itself must come from the academic community, for if higher education cannot draw direction from all its components, it will surely wander and be lost.

Any coherent, comprehensive posture to promote the general welfare of higher education will involve compromises. And when one looks at the program for regeneration, one realizes that these compromises will be difficult to develop and perhaps even more difficult to accept. Faculty will agonize over but, in view of changing demographic and socio-economic alignments, dare not ignore a review of tenure, hiring, evaluation, promotion, and other personnel practices. Administrators will need the utmost ingenuity in the search for even greater flexibility in the use of money, facilities, and professional and staff time. Faculty and administrators must both accept the responsibility for creative but prudent innovation in curricula, credit structures, admissions standards, degree requirements, teaching loads, research priorities, grading systems, graduate and undergraduate college structures, and the traditional concept and boundaries of disciplines. In all of these actions, we members of the higher education community must seek to preserve the spirit of higher education—to promote the life of the mind—even as we negotiate its forms and substance. And, disagreeable as we may find the task ahead, we must undertake it, or surely circumstances will impose the decisions of others upon us.

The challenge to higher education today recalls the old story from Sufic wisdom about the blind men and the elephant. Once upon a time there was a village beyond the city of Ghor, in which all the inhabitants were blind. One day an elephant wandered by chance into the village, causing much panic and destruction. Never having known an elephant before, and anxious to discover what had wrought so much havoc, some men of the village set out with their dogs to track down the strange intruder and find out what they could. They came upon the elephant resting placidly some distance from the town and, not knowing the form or shape of the beast, they groped sightlessly, gathering information by touching some part of it. Each thought he knew something of value because he could feel a part. They returned to their village, and their fellow citizens immediately clustered about, eager to learn the truth. One of the explorers, whose hand had reached an ear, told them: "It is a large, rough thing, wide and broad, like a rug." The one who had felt the trunk said: "No. I have the real facts about it. It is like a straight and hollow pipe, awful and destructive." A third man, who had felt its legs, said: "You are both wrong. It is mighty and firm, like a pillar."

As with many situations in life, the outline of the forest is clear enough when seen from the proper perspective, but its shape is indiscernible when viewed from the vantage point of a single tree. We will discover what the "elephant" truly is only through communication and consensus. But at that point, any and every one of us will be able to champion our colleges and universities, for we will have forged St. George's lance and shield together.

8

Agents for Social Change?

The Black Experience

HERMAN B. SMITH, JR.

I REPRESENT social change. The story of Herman B. Smith, Jr., gives testimony to some degree of success, in fact conspicuous success, to the achievement of a basic and defensible goal of American institutions of higher education.

I am literate and articulate. I enjoy Jackson Pollock as well as Charles White and Pierre Renoir. The works of Bach and Rachmaninoff represent my favorite music. I was born a poor black boy. My father and mother suffered for the primary and secondary education of their son; I witnessed all the hardships of life in a southern city during the 1930s and 1940s pursuing a classical education in an inadequately equipped small schoolhouse. To a considerable degree by chance, I found my way to Knoxville College, where dedicated scholars fed, clothed, and taught a few young black men and women of promise and pushed them on to graduate schools such as the University of Wisconsin.

> I, too, sing America. I am the darker brother. They sent me to eat in the kitchen when company came, but I laughed, an' ate well, and grew strong. Today, I sit at the table when company comes. Nobody dares

say to me, "Eat in the kitchen" now. Besides, they see how beautiful I am and are ashamed—I, too, am America.[1]

How appropriate are Langston Hughes' words!

Today there are monumental social differences between the few blacks who made it and the many who did not in terms of contributions to society, life-styles, and aspirations. There is no doubt in my mind and yours that higher education made a difference.

My position is that the American goal of eroding and eliminating race as a barrier to achievement is one to which the institutions of higher education are morally and legally committed; that the colleges and universities have made significant strides in the eradication of this barrier by transforming individuals into useful elements of American society; and that black colleges and universities have historically rendered miraculous services toward the achievement of this goal.

Moral and legal commitment to social change

My argument is brief but persistent on the moral and legal commitment of colleges and universities to the elimination of racial prejudice in our society. We drew our beginning from the principle that states, "all men are created equal."[2] No law in America—absolutely no law—is recognized if it is in violation of the U. S. Constitution's Thirteenth Amendment outlawing slavery; of the Fourteenth Amendment, which provides equal protection for the life, liberty, and property of all U. S. citizens; or of the Fifteenth Amendment, which ensures the right of all U. S. citizens to vote regardless of race, color, or creed.[3] We live by and die for these words.

It became necessary for the President's Commission on National Goals to reaffirm this commitment as we moved into the difficult 1960s. Goal number two of the fifteen goals for America as prepared by the Commission reads:

> Vestiges of religious prejudice, handicaps to women, and, most importantly, discrimination on the basis of race must be recognized as morally wrong, economically wasteful, and in many respects dangerous. In this decade we must sharply lower these stubborn barriers.
>
> Respect for the individual means respect for *every* individual. Every

1. Langston Hughes, "I, Too," *Anthology of American Negro Literature,* ed. V. F. Calverton (New York: Modern Library, 1929), pp. 210–11 (paraphrased).
2. *Declaration of Independence,* 1776.
3. *U. S. Constitution.*

man and woman must have equal rights before the law, and an equal opportunity to vote and hold office, to be educated, to get a job and to be promoted when qualified, to buy a home, to participate fully in community affairs.[4]

This American creed, according to Gunnar Myrdal, poses an American dilemma: ". . . the American thinks, talks, and acts under the influence of high national and Christian precepts, but on the other hand . . . all sorts of miscellaneous wants, impulses, and habits dominate his outlook." Included in these are personal and local interests; economic, social, and sexual jealousies; considerations of community prestige and conformity; and group prejudices against particular persons or types of people.[5]

The social condition that has tested all American institutions has been institutionalized racial prejudice. Colleges and universities have met this challenge with a great degree of excellence by preparing blacks to assume professional careers that help to prove human worth; by deepening the intellectual desires and sharpening the skill of mastering information and knowledge;[6] by promoting objective research, which proves racial prejudice to be unfounded intellectually and scientifically; by modifying the American dilemma to afford more than lip-service to equal opportunity and affirmative action; and by promoting changes in white social values in regard to racial prejudice.

Changes in institutionalized racism

The quality of performance has continued to improve. An assessment of the quantity, however, reveals less real progress and suggests implications for the future role of colleges and universities as the United States struggles to achieve its goals.

A review of the saga of black natural scientists with the earned Ph.D., for example, reveals that the first black American to earn a Ph.D. in the natural sciences was Edward S. Bouchet, who earned a Ph.D. in physics from Yale University in 1876. By 1900 there was yet only one American black with a Ph.D. in the natural sciences. There were 13

4. President's Commission on National Goals, *Goals for Americans: Programs for Action in the Sixties* (Englewood Cliffs, N.J.: Prentice Hall, 1960), pp. 3–4.

5. Gunnar Myrdal, *An American Dilemma: The Negro Problem and Modern Democracy* (New York: Harper and Brothers, 1942), p. xlvii.

6. Douglas H. Heath, "What the Enduring Effects of Higher Education Tell Us About a Liberal Education," *Journal of Higher Education,* March/April 1976, pp. 173–90.

by 1930; 119 by 1943; 200 by 1950; 850 by 1972;[7] and 332 were awarded between 1973 and 1976. Thus, a total of 1,173 was awarded since 1876. Whites earned 31,029 Ph.D.'s in the natural sciences between 1973–76.[8] Therefore, the total number of doctorates in the natural sciences awarded to blacks in more than 100 years is less than 4 percent of the number awarded to whites in the three years, 1973–76.

Each year more doctoral degrees in the natural sciences are awarded to foreign nationals than to black Americans. In 1971, 15 percent of the doctorates in the natural sciences were awarded to foreign nationals, while less than 1 percent were awarded to black Americans.[9]

I want to note progress unless I am accused by Mr. Ben J. Wattenberg, author of *The Real America,* of engaging in liberal rhetoric on black progress.[10] It is observed that during the three years 1973–76, there was a 38 percent increase in the earned Ph.D. awarded to blacks, and no one can deny that this is progress. Note well, however, that of the 182 black doctorates in the natural sciences awarded by 150 Ph.D.-granting institutions in 1972, 29 were granted by two historically black institutions. During this year, 13,432 white doctorates in the natural sciences were produced. This reemphasizes the fact that the total number of blacks with the earned Ph.D. in the natural sciences is less than a thimbleful by anyone's measurement, and only in a small way contributes to the realization of the American goal of equal opportunity for all Americans.

I think that I have said enough about numbers to make my point that even though the percentage of black students enrolled in institutions of higher education has tripled in a decade, we have not made real progress toward our goal if the case of the natural scientists prevails, that is if in 1976 only 9.3 percent, or 1,062,000 of all students enrolled in 3,000 institutions of higher learning are black, and 30 percent or 300,000 of these blacks are enrolled in 113 historically black colleges and universities.[11]

7. Horace M. Bond, *Black American Scholars: A Study of Their Beginnings* (Detroit: Balamp, 1972).

8. "Fact-File," *Chronicle of Higher Education,* March 27, 1978, p. 18.

9. Ford Foundation, *A Survey of Black American Doctorates* (New York: Ford Foundation, 1972).

10. Ben J. Wattenberg, *The Real America: A Surprising Examination of the State of the Union* (New York: Doubleday, 1974), pp. 124–51.

11. "Minority Enrollment Rose 23.2 Pct. in Two Years: 9.3 Pct. of All Students in 1976 Were Black According to Survey by Civil Rights Agency," *Chronicle of Higher Education,* March 20, 1978, pp. 16–20.

Higher education has made me proud and sometimes boastful even to the point of ebulliency. Therefore, I must note some of the achievements of that handful of natural scientists—colleagues whom I know well.

Dr. Lafayette Frederick—mycologist, Ph.D. from Washington State University, member of the Southeast Forestry Research Advancement Commission, Research Grant Review Science Programs in Predominantly Black Colleges for the Natural Science Foundation. Dr. Frederick has served as advisor to twenty-seven black students who have received Ph.D.'s in botany, microbiology, and molecular biology.

One of the notable black contributors in the area of chemistry is Dr. Percy Julian, who synthesized physostigmine, a drug used to treat glaucoma. He perfected the process for extracting sterols from soybeans, and thus contributed to the lowered cost of cortisone and other sterol derivatives, making the treatment of such ailments as arthritis more accessible to sufferers.

Dr. J. Ernest Wilkins, Jr., a renowned mathematician, also trained in physics, is the black man who worked on the Manhattan Project. Today there are fewer than 100 blacks in America who hold the Ph.D. in mathematics.

Dr. Booker Whatley has lectured in the Middle East and Africa on plant breeding and other subjects in horticulture. Dr. Whatley does his work at Tuskegee Institute and, like George Washington Carver, he swims against the tides as he pursues research in agricultural science.

I could go on to talk about these few men of great distinction. Dr. George R. Curruthers, for example, is one of four blacks to hold the Ph.D. in astronomy. He heads the Ultraviolet Astronomy Section of the Naval Research Laboratories' Space Science Division, and was named most promising and outstanding astronomer under thirty-five years of age by the National Society of Astronomers in 1973.[12]

It should be noted that more than 75 percent of all black natural scientists with the earned Ph.D. are employed by 113 historically black colleges and universities. The professional yield of these scientists has been prolific and of the highest quality. Unfortunately, outlets for these black men have in the past been restricted and discouraging.[13]

12. F. C. Richardson, "A Quarter Century of the Black Experience in the Natural Sciences, 1950–1974," *Negro Educational Review*, April, 1976, pp. 144–54.

13. Ibid., p. 146.

Colleges and universities: agencies of social change?

Without a doubt, a resounding "yes" is the answer to the question, "Are colleges and universities agencies of social change?" These institutions have been agencies of social change since their inception, and they must continue to be such.

The United States has been confronted with the single most important social issue of the century: the need to eradicate racial prejudice. Racial prejudice through the years has gnawed at the roots of the tree of democracy.

Colleges and universities have been the most successful agents of change in the United States and have made significant strides in deinstitutionalizing racial prejudice. As I review the tasks of yesterday, today, and tomorrow, my challenge to colleges and universities is as follows: (1) Increase the quantity of educated blacks. This will have direct and profound impact on the momentum of social change in the nation. Numbers are important. (2) Refrain from compromising the existing commitment to high standards for higher education. But don't play games with blacks. Higher education has the know-how so to perform. (3) Recognize the intrinsic worth of the historically black colleges and universities and the roles they have played and must continue to play in advancing social equality to all Americans. In fact it is most appropriate to urge that the continued and expanded partnership between historically white and black colleges and universities be maintained and improved. (4) Move beyond the immediate campus and help to facilitate achievement of social justice and equality in education, in housing, and, most important, in employment. Yield no quarter in the services and in the important task of interpreting widely and repetitively the goals of higher education, the potential of higher education, and the yield of higher education. The results of such procedures will be substantial.

What happens to a dream deferred? Remember that the American dream is our dream.

The Indian Experience

MARIAN M. HERSRUD

WHY should educators in the 1970s question the role of colleges and universities as agents of social change? I share the philosophy of John Dewey, who wrote, "Education is the fundamental method of social progress and reform."[1] But what kind of progress and reform? That question is most perplexing in the realm of education for minorities. If we state simply that progress is upward mobility in white society, we assume that all minorities wish to adopt the white culture, and this is not the basic assumption of all Indian students.

South Dakota is one of only eighteen states that have Indian populations of more than 10,000, and that sounds like a small drop in the bucket of education's woes and worries; but the number of Indian students on the campuses has risen from 2,358 in 1967 to 25,000 in 1977,[2] and this number will increase as more Indians realize that they can get through college and thereby do something for their own people. If people in all areas of education consider colleges and universities as agents of social progress and reform, the non-Indian community should take a good look at a civilization that is 25,000 years older than Christendom; and that look must not be stereotyped, biased, or superficial.

Indian myths and mysticism

People are to a great extent what other people think they are. Indian people have moved from being considered, as Annie D. Tallent described them in 1899, "graceless savages," "relentless and bloody Sioux," and "invaders"[3] to being dealt with now in myths. One of these myths, which must be dispelled, is that Uncle Sam supports the Indian totally, that the Indian receives a weekly stipend for doing nothing and that any Indian student can have a free ride on the college train with first-class accommodations. It just is not so. While government grants

1. John Dewey, "My Pedagogic Creed" (originally published in 1897), in *School and Society* (Boston: D. C. Heath, 1962), p. 494.
2. Bureau of Indian Affairs, in "Indian Education" (David J. Mathieu, Center of Indian Studies, Black Hills State College, Spearfish, South Dakota, 1976), mimeographed, p. 276.
3. *The Black Hills or Last Hunting Grounds of the Dakotahs* (originally published 1899, Sioux Falls, S.D.: Brevet Press, 1974).

and loans have increased in recent years, the average Indian family lives at a level of poverty such that it cannot ensure the added dollars needed for a college education.

Another myth that embarrasses the Indian person is the sudden ascent into a kind of Carlos Castaneda creation, endowed with cosmic mysticism. While some medicine men do possess incredible powers of spirit, the average Indian is not at one with the supernatural. If that were so, the dropout rate among Indian students would be far less.

Who, then, is the Indian student, and what does he or she expect from a college education? First of all, Indian life is not compartmentalized. One cannot study any aspect of Indian life without involving the total Indian culture. John F. Bryde of the school of education at the University of South Dakota expressed this all-inclusiveness as follows:

> If one would walk up to an old time Indian living today and ask him why the Indian people do a certain action—for instance, why Indian children don't "rock the boat" or stick their heads above the crowd—he would give you an answer founded NOT in psychology but in philosophy. For instance, in response to the above question, he might say that, since all of us are ONE, a person doesn't fight against himself by competing to win just for himself. You have to think about that for awhile to appreciate the depth of the old person's response.
>
> The reason that an old timer would give a philosophical answer to a psychological question is that, even for convenience, the Indian mind does not separate branches of knowledge. Reflecting their view of reality, all knowledge is ONE. In order to know Indian psychology, then, one must know Indian philosophy—or the great Indian value system.[4]

This basic noncompartmentalization follows the Indian student into the structured classroom, which offers science first period and history the second. Values are already flying at each other.

Wanblee: victory and defeat

I would like to take a close look at an example of Indian schooling, in Wanblee, South Dakota, in the heart of the Pine Ridge reservation. "Wanblee" means "eagle" in the Sioux language. Sacred to the Oglalas because he flies close to Wakan Tonka, God, the eagle is the symbol of victory. But the Wanblee school system can mean defeat for little Mary

---

4. John F. Bryde, "Indian Psychology," in *The University of South Dakota Bulletin, Institute of Indian Studies* (Vermillion, S.D., May 1978), p. 2.

Driving Horse. The school itself, built with government funds, is the envy of many white schools, but Mary's teachers may not be. The better teachers shy away from "the res," as they call the reservation, and those who do come remain only a short time. Their enthusiasm soon gives way to frustration because of communication gaps between white faculty members and Indian students and their families. Teaching standards drop in proportion to that frustration.

Communication gaps widen as Mary studies American history. In the Indian traditions of exact repetition and eloquence, Mary has learned her Indian history at home. At school she reads, "The Indians had met the fate of inferior peoples and weak nations . . .,"[5] and she soon comprehends that "how it was" as her parents taught is not "how it was" in school. Mary knows that someone is lying, and she may lose her respect for classroom authority.

Mary will struggle through on an average of five grades doing battle with a second language. If English is spoken at home, it is usually ungrammatical and halting, and few reservation teachers are bilingual.

If Mary can survive twelve years of disappointment and discrimination, she will receive her diploma and be ready for college. But Mary didn't make it; she quit in despair at the end of fifth grade.

Bill One Hawk did make it. I will follow his progress now as he leaves the reservation and goes off to an institution of higher education. His first contact on campus will be the Indian Student Affairs office, if there is one. The counselor, an Indian himself who understands Bill's problems, if he's lucky, welcomes him. "Hello, Bill. Here are fifty million grant and loan forms to fill out." If Bill can make sense of that tangle, he's already Phi Beta Kappa material!

He will be noticed in the classroom, and his professor will react in one of two ways. He will groan inwardly, knowing that Bill has not received adequate preparation, that he is in college on a government loan, probably because the college wants to raise its enrollment figures, and that he will not respond in class. Even if the professor knows that Indian kids have been taught to be seen and not heard, he will not know how to deal with the problem.

The second possible reaction of teacher to Indian student, though outwardly humanistic, is even worse. This professor "digs Indians." In Indian circles he is known as the "bleeding heart." Bleeding Heart will empa-

5. George M. Stephenson, *American History Since 1865* (New York: Harper & Brothers, 1939), p. 79.

thize and sympathize to such a degree that he will give Bill a passing grade no matter how he performs in class. He may give Bill college credit for remedial work, which demeans the college experience and robs him of his pride. Thus Bill has not learned what it means to compete in the white world, his diploma is a mockery, and he can now add another verse to his song, "It's Not My Fault."

If there is a department of Indian studies on campus, Bill may enroll, hoping to find a meaningful transition into white society. But the standard department will not help him, with its watered-down, hit-and-miss course work, which in some cases may teach him to become an Indian. Beadwork 204 is not instruction; it is insulting!

After the first week of classes, Bill may reassess his priorities, and any family activity on the reservation will seem more attractive than classes on campus. Absenteeism is the cause of many failures, and it is not enough to shrug it off with "Oh, well, that's the Indian way." If Bill's college experience is to be successful, reasons for his absences must be pursued.

Drugs and alcohol will have special appeal for the unhappy Indian student. Bill will be strongly tempted to take a negative social trip.

If Bill is able to cope with all of his problems, he will rank in only the twenty-sixth percentile of Indian students who complete their first year of college. Seventy-four percent of his Indian classmates will have thrown in the academic towel and retreated to the reservation.

This is Bill One Hawk. Now, what does he expect from his college education? He expects to master the tools he needs to assist his people when he returns to the reservation to work and live. He expects to master the tools he needs to make it in the white world. The goals vary. How can they be achieved?

Dispersed learning on the reservation

The reservation college is one answer to how Bill's goals can be achieved, and South Dakota's Oglala Sioux Community College is an excellent example. The college consists of the Lakota Higher Education Center and Sinte Gleska College. They are community colleges in the true sense, because they are locally controlled by Indian boards, and they address in their vocational offerings reservation manpower needs. Both Pine Ridge and Rosebud reservations use learning centers rather than traditional campuses, because the reservations are made up of such large areas with scattered, small population centers. One-track dirt roads and howling blizzards also make it difficult to organize a central campus. This system of education centers is called dispersed learning and it works. Associate of Arts degrees in nursing, general studies, education and business are accredited through the University of South Dakota, Black Hills State College, and the Regents of Higher Education. A highlight of my term as regent in 1970 was to welcome tribal leaders and Bureau of Indian Affairs officials as they presented the Sicangu people's request for our endorsement of their new venture. Our enthusiasm has grown into involvement, not only accreditation. The regents held their August meeting this year on the campus of Sinte Gleska College. The state gives no financial support, however. South Dakota has no tax jurisdiction on the reservation, and too many state legislators are caught up in the myth of unlimited federal funding for the Indian people.

The reservation colleges have many positive side effects. The college climate, dispersed though it is, offers concrete evidence of something beyond high school. Functioning also as community centers, the colleges serve in many areas of adult and continuing education by offering adult basic education, enrichment courses, and the how-to's that are desperately needed in rural areas. The students are predominantly Indian; culture shock does not exist.

And this brings me to a large minus if Bill One Hawk wants upward mobility in a white world. Has he simply postponed facing the non-Indian community, or will his college experience, albeit on the reservation, give him that needed sense of pride and self-worth? Answers vary according to individual needs and abilities, personalities, and motivations.

The Indian problem is the white problem

If the reservation college is not the answer for Bill, his only other resource remains the traditional college campus; thus the Indian problem becomes the white problem. For the present, Bill will have to cope with his lack of adequate college preparation, but much can be done with in-service training and workshops for all levels of faculty members who are currently working with Indian students.

Counselors of Indian students must not only understand Indian ways; they must also recognize that continued counseling will be needed. It cannot stop after the first week of school.

Because Indian families have strong family ties, Bill's parents must be encouraged to know campus life and to understand its demands upon their son. "Indian Culture Week," complete with powwows involving the family, might precede that first trauma of adjustment to class routine.

Much more needs to be done in bilingual-bicultural education, particularly for future elementary and secondary teachers. A smattering of Sioux and a strong emphasis on bicultural studies are rewarding, not only for that future student but for the future teacher as well. My participation in sun dances, powwows, and pipe ceremonies has enriched my life; and when a wasicu (white person) can laugh with Jim Robideau, when he says with a wink, "Custer wore Arrow shirts," new avenues of communication between the races are open.

Colleges and universities must find this path to mutual understanding and respect, and they can find it if they develop a new generation of teachers. Many Indian students have already discovered that they can attend a non-Indian college without losing their "Indianness," but they need faculty members who are willing to change their teaching methods and some of their value systems. All of this is, of course, learner-centered education, which attracts much lip service but little commitment.

Philip Werdell wrote,

> The greatest public service higher education can perform is to develop people prepared to help solve society's emerging problems—who can articulate their own needs, who can understand the needs of others, and who can thus go on to create new goals and develop new forms of learning and doing.[6]

Colleges are indeed agencies for social change.

6. Philip Werdell, "Futurism and the Reform of Higher Education," in *Learning For Tomorrow*, ed. Alvin Toffler (New York: Vintage Books, 1974), p. 286.

Higher Education's Social Role

CHARLES FRANKEL

SHOULD colleges and universities be expected to be agencies for social change? One of the astonishing aspects of this question is the willingness of people to debate it heatedly while treating the multitude of other questions on which it depends as though they had already received clear and cogent answers. But they have not. Let me list a few such questions as samples of the many that could be asked.

What is social change? New techniques in advertising? Beatlemania? A widespread return to pentecostal religion? Reduction of the tax revenues available to government? Or women's rights, social equality, new forms of economic planning? And why one and not the other? In sum, what kind of social change do "we" desire?

Who are the "we" who are to make this choice? Is it the academic community—students, teachers, professors? Why is it expected that this so-called "community"—not renowned for its ability to achieve a consensus on any issue—should be able to agree on a matter of momentous significance such as the direction that social change should take? If consensus is not expected, what are the procedures that will ensure fair representation and selection of people with the authority to act in the name of a university community? And what is the authority for assigning to university communities the moral and political responsibilities here presumed?

A different assumption, of course, may underlie the view that colleges and universities should act as agents of social change: it is that they should be instruments of the external society. But if so, of what elements in that society will they be the instrument, and whose opinions shall be taken to count? Assuming that these decisions will not be capricious or intuitive, is it to be presumed that colleges and universities will act as agents of courts and legislatures, or the bureaucracies legally empowered to speak for the public will? But is it compatible with academic freedom and autonomy to allow such governmental entities to determine the character and objectives of higher education and research? And will it help higher education or hurt it to introduce systematically into college and university governing boards the political quarrels that rend the outside community?

Moreover, there are practical questions to be asked. Assuming agreement on the desirable direction of social change, why should colleges and universities be the agents of this change? Why should anyone suppose that professors of English or students of theology or sociology— to say nothing of sophomores barely released from the parental roof and still struggling with the mysteries of the simple English sentence— are competent to perform this task? Moreover, are these members of the academic community not in a curious situation with regard to the exercise of this function? They are neither officials specifically chosen to act as agents of the community, nor simply private citizens exercising their personal right to spend their own money and use their own time to advance their conception of the social good. They are using their time on the job, and working with other people's money, usually taxpayers'.

Consider, as a final example, a quite elementary question: Why a concern with social change? Why not a concern with social stability, or with preservation of such excellence as exists against corrupting influences? What is wrong, indeed, with the status quo? Admittedly, it has its blemishes, but, if we must choose among general abstract propositions, it is no more foolish to believe that change will generally be for the worse than to assume that change is generally for the better.

The function of education—it has been said on innumerable occasions—is to teach people to adjust to change. Why? Some changes are lethal. People should surely be educated, if possible, to recognize and shun these changes. Other changes are such that no honorable person would accept them. Does education have no responsibility to teach people when adjustment to change would be mere cowardice or adventurism? Any man or woman of independent judgment will recognize a need to distinguish between the desirable and the undesirable, to work for some sort of change, and to be a fierce member of the resistance with regard to others. Is it not a mistake, then—indeed, a form of moral evasion or obtuseness—to inscribe the motto "social change" so conspicuously on the banners of higher education?

Why formal schooling?

I have asked these questions, I confess, with a certain intellectual malice, but my intent is simply to clear the air. As it happens, I believe that colleges and universities do have obligations with regard to social change; indeed, whether they have obligations or not they are fundamentally involved in processes of social change, serving both as reflections of such processes and as motive forces behind them. But a sane approach to the issues depends on not treating difficult questions as though they did not exist or as though the answers to them were already established. Let me indulge, then, in some reflections on the philosophical and historical background of the issues we are examining.

It is useful to begin by bearing in mind the special roles that formal schooling plays in a society. Education, broadly speaking, is of course not the same as schooling. It is a universal and inescapable feature of human existence, inseparable in every society from family and religion, games, work, the hunt, the rites associated with birth, growth, and death, the simple intercourse of daily life. Man is a culture-dependent animal, a teaching animal, a learning animal. The individual human being's education (and miseducation) takes place whether or not anyone is deliberately thinking about it. Schooling is only one form of education. It is a part of education that is deliberate and organized. But even in societies that devote much time and many resources to the process of schooling, its influence is small in comparison with all the other educational processes that affect human personality and conduct.

Nevertheless, schooling does have a considerable importance, and it is worth asking what conditions lead societies to engage in it. I suggest there are at least five kinds of circumstance that generate formal schooling.

The first is the rise of systems of class stratification and occupational specialization. These generate traditions of special knowledge or treasured values, which are associated with the existence and doings of particular classes, crafts, or professions, and which are deemed to be so important as to justify special schools to ensure their continuity across the generations. This movement toward formal schooling is usually strengthened by the desire to control access to positions of power, security, or special benefit. Thus the mysteries associated with membership in medieval guilds; thus the emergence of schools in the early modern period for the education, under protected conditions, of the children of bourgeois families.

A second condition conducive to the development of formal schooling is the emergence of an awareness in society that there is a gap between its inherited lore and techniques and new knowledge and techniques, practical or theoretical. The advent of Euclidean geometry presented such a situation to the ancient Athenians, as did the development of the arts of rhetoric and argument in public assemblies and courts of law. Schools emerge as places where the young can, as it were, be saved from their informal education—where they can be trained more sharply and systematically, and where the information and skills imparted to them can reflect the process of criticism of received dispensation which is taking place in society.

A third reason is the emergence of convictions such goals as social concord or economic efficiency require that education can no longer be left to the informal educative processes of work and play. General literacy, for example, may come to be discerned as a desideratum of education, above and beyond special skills associated, say, with carpentering, hunting, or the like. Schools are thus created to provide education in materials and skills that require special and concentrated attention.

Fourth, schools have emerged in response to a conviction that fundamental values of a society, necessary to its strength or its basic survival, must somehow be transmitted either to a selected group or to citizens at large, and that the family, the marketplace, the workplace, the church, the theater can no longer perform these functions adequately, but need the support of schools. Plato, the first systematic philosopher of education in the Western tradition, developed his ideas for the special schooling of the city of Athens' guardian class after coming to the conclusion that the established institutions for transmitting the civic virtues necessary to Athenian civilization were themselves in the grip of the forces responsible for Athens' decadence, and were no longer capable of performing their assigned role.

The fifth circumstance, which is perhaps really a corollary of the fourth, is the emergence of changed perceptions about the role and power of the family. "Are you going to send your boy to college?" Mr. Hennessy once asked Mr. Dooley. "I can't do anything else," Mr. Dooley replied. "At the age when a boy is fit to be sent to college, he's noi fit to be kept at home." We have contrived in the modern world, without aiming at such a result, to channel large numbers of physically adult young people into a waiting period, an in-between status, neither children nor grown-up. We call this phenomenon and its attendant tremors adolescence, and homes have not been quite up to the task of containing it.

There are other circumstances, too, that have reduced the role of the family as an educational influence. Schools grew in number in the period of early capitalism, for example, because newly rich families perceived that they were incapable of teaching their children the manners and diction that would allow them to move at ease among people of the better sort. Similarly, school systems have grown in size and complexity, and in the responsibilities assigned to them, as women of the working class (and now of the middle class) have moved into the labor market. Industrial society, which has promoted social mobility and separated the home from the workplace, has created the conditions that have required or invited the state to step in as a custodial and educative agent. In the *école maternelle,* the grammar school, the public high school, the great state universities, the lineaments of the contemporary welfare state can be discerned as far back as a hundred or a hundred and fifty years ago.

The school's place in society

This is simply a sketch, but I hope that enough has been said to allow two fundamental themes to emerge. First, the conditions I have cited as producing a movement toward organized schooling have one element in common. They are signs of social change, reactions to it, expressions of a desire to protect oneself and one's children against its effects or of a wish to advance it and profit from it. Schools in this sense are elements in the process of social change. They witness to its effects, and they represent attempts to regulate it and control its consequences.

Second, schools are crossroads of competing purposes. They exist to protect the privileged and also to give opportunities to the hitherto disadvantaged; to transmit the received lore of society and also to break away from that lore; to advance the purposes of specific trades and professions and to limit access to them, and also to give these trades and professions a more public perspective and sense of commitment; to assist the family and compete with the family; to shore up the established values of the community, and also to put these values under pressure. Each of these reasons for introducing schools into society has its own dynamic; it introduces demands on schools, not usually in harmony, with the other demands. A central function of educational philosophy and, at another level, of educational politics and educational administration, is to sort out these demands in each generation, to assign relative weights to them, and to seek some coherent way of responding to them together.

I speak of schools, and most of what I have said applies to all schools, including colleges and universities. Institutions of higher education, however, are perhaps peculiarly susceptible to certain kinds of dilemma, especially when they function in societies that have great social mobility, political freedom, and intellectual liberty. They train people for favored positions in society and are under the twin and often competing demands to open up the channels of social promotion and to train people capable of performing important tasks in a competent fashion. To have a chance to be trained as a lawyer or doctor, for example, is to have a chance to achieve substantial personal benefits, and we can think of a system of admissions to professional schools as a system for the distribution of social benefits. But doctors and lawyers have patients and clients, so admission to the professions can also be viewed as a method of assuring competent social services rather than as a distribution of benefits.

Institutions of higher education, furthermore, are embedded in the research and development sector of industrial societies. Their task is to criticize received dispensations, to innovate, to disturb the established mentality. They are, in all probability, the major agents of social change in these societies—at any rate, of those social changes that are produced by scientific theories, by technology, by the critique of law and politics, by the advance of medicine, and by new interpretations of the cultural and moral heritage. Yet at the same time, institutions of higher education also have the task of serving as symbols and exemplars of cultural and social continuity. They are expected, by those who support them, to train the people who will maintain the social fabric.

Are colleges and universities, then, agents of social change? Should they be? The questions, I suggest, are more complex than polemical approaches suggest, and the answers must be too. The modern French university, for example, is a product of the Napoleonic reforms. It was conceived as an agent for recruiting and training the teachers, scientists, lawyers, doctors, administrators who would reorganize France, make its economy and laws and citizens more rational, create the wealth that would support the state and its international preeminence, and open the paths that would permit ability to rise and be recognized and used. Was social change contemplated? Of course. Profound social change. But by the same token, these universities were instruments of conservation. Their purpose was to give support to the existing regime, to strengthen its foundations, to provide it with its officer class.

The American land-grant college has not been different. It was intended to change the character of agriculture and rural life in the United States; it was an instrument, it might be said, of the metropolitan culture. State universities, too, with their more generous admissions policies and variegated degree programs contemplated changes in the social structure and the existing system of privileges and preferments. And the great research universities have enjoyed their academic freedom largely as a result of the public acceptance (often grudging, somewhat unsteady, but nevertheless long-lived) of the proposition that American society could not rest on its conventions or its past successes, but that it needed new and troublesome ideas and a leadership trained in independence and habits of inquiry. Yet the American habit of looking upon higher educational institutions as instruments of social change is part of a larger habit of regarding them as instruments of social stabilization. A constitutional democracy, in the habitual American perspective, depends for its health and continuity on its capacity to maintain social mobility and a capacity for peaceful reform. Universities are crucial to these purposes—agents of socal change and of social conservation both.

Against this background, are there any general lessons that seem to emerge? The heart of the matter is that (except for very small institutions associated with specific religious sects) colleges and universities are crossroads where competing purposes meet and different constituencies make legitimate demands. This complex and highly dissensual sort of institution has nevertheless been assigned a distinctive and indispensable role in the polity   the husbanding and cultivating of the nation's intellectual resources, the transmission of a cultural heritage in an enlightened manner, and the pursuit of new knowledge, let the chips fall where they may. The invitation to them to express collective opinions about such matters as the propriety of South Africa's policies or Equal Rights Amendment boycotts should therefore be rejected. Colleges and universities have a long-term business that should not be compromised by politicizing and moralizing. Indeed colleges and universities—and, more specifically, the individual members of their faculties—can make a special claim to be listened to only so long as their aspiration to independence and integrity is not subject to serious challenge. Educational institutions cheapen themselves and degrade the currency of their intellectual life if they are captured by this political faction or that, or if they express corporate opinions each month on remote and complex problems of which the great majority of the faculties and student bodies cannot be expected to have more than a sloganeer's or advertising man's comprehension.

It is not when colleges and universities stick to their central business that they ignore moral issues or retreat from reality; it is when they stand forth to render collective judgments on matters beyond their collective ken that they behave irresponsibly and show themselves in the grip of unexamined ideologies. The professors in Germany who accepted the Nazi regime were unfaithful to principles essential to the maintenance of honest conditions of work in their own backyards. Such honest conditions of work require, precisely, that a university in its corporate life be nonpolitical, leaving the individuals who compose it to make their own independent decisions about how to exercise their rights as citizens.

Bibliography

THIS bibliography *supplements* the one included in *Federal Regulation and Higher Education* by Louis W. Bender, published early in 1977 as ERIC/Higher Education Research Report No. 1, 1977, by the American Association for Higher Education for the ERIC Clearinghouse on Higher Education ($3.50 from AAHE, One Dupont Circle, Suite 780, Washington, D.C. 20036). Thus, nothing is included in this list that was in the 1977 bibliography. Users should also note that both lists are selected from considerably larger files of documents related to the topic, most of which are included in the ERIC system. Margot Saunders Eddy of ERIC provided a printout of around 300 ERIC items with their descriptive paragraphs; selections from this list were supplemented by other documents from several sources. Documents with numbers preceded by ED are available in microfiche or hard copy from ERIC. Consult the ERIC catalogs, available in most university libraries, for ordering information and prices.

"A Call to Trustees." *AGB Reports,* March/April 1978, pp. 3–9.

American Association of Presidents of Independent Colleges and Universities. *Private Higher Education: The Job Ahead.* Malibu, California: Pepperdine University, 1977.

Anderson, Richard E. "The Paradox of Pluralism." *Change,* May 1977, pp. 50–51.

Andringa, Robert C. "Capitol Hill—An Insider's View." *AGB Reports,* September/October 1976, pp. 10–16.

Arnstein, George E. "Fighting Fraud in Education." *American Education,* April 1977, pp. 27–30.

Bell, Terrel H. *Increasing Access to Postsecondary Education—The Federal Role.* Geneva, Switzerland: International Conference on Education of the International Bureau of Education, August 1975.

———. *Morality and Citizenship Education: Whose Responsibility? Planning for Moral/Citizenship Education, Occasional Paper No. 1.* Philadelphia: Research for Better Schools, Inc., 1976.

Bender, Louis W. *Federal Regulation and Higher Education.* ERIC/HE Research Report No. 1. Washington, D.C.: American Association on Higher Education, March 1977.

Bender, Louis W., and Breuder, Robert L. "The Federal/State Paperwork Menace." *Community College Review,* Summer 1977, pp. 16–22.

Benezet, Louis T. *Private Higher Education and Public Funding.* ERIC/ HE Research Report No. 5. Washington, D.C.: American Association for Higher Education, 1976.

Binkley, Max A. *Cost of Federal Research Performed by the Universities: A Call for Equity.* Washington, D.C.: National Association of College and University Business Officers, April 1977.

Birnbaum, Norman. "Higher Education and the Federal Government." *Educational Record,* vol. 57, no. 4, pp. 225–31.

Bonham, George W., et al. *In the Public Interest.* New Rochelle, N.Y.: Change Magazine Press, November 1978.

Boyer, Ernest L. "The Federal Stake in a Learning Society: An Interview with Ernest L. Boyer." *Change,* May 1978, pp. 21–25.

Breneman, David, and Finn, Chester E., Jr., eds. *Public Policy and Private Higher Education.* Washington, D.C.: The Brookings Institution, 1978.

Budig, Gene A., ed. *Dollars and Sense: Budgeting for Today's Campus.* Chicago: College and University Business Press, 1972.

Burke, John D., ed. *Proceedings of the National Conference on Public Service and the Federal-University Partnership.* Athens, Ga.: University of Georgia, 1978.

Callan, Patrick M., and Jonsen, Richard W. "The State Role." *New Directions for Higher Education,* Spring 1976, pp. 25–34.

Carnegie Commission on Higher Education. *Governance of Higher Education: Six Priority Problems.* New York: McGraw-Hill, 1973.

Carnegie Council on Policy Studies in Higher Education. *Federal Reorganization: Education and Scholarship.* Berkeley: Carnegie Council on Policy Studies in Higher Education, 1977.

Carnegie Council on Policy Studies in Higher Education. *The States and Private Higher Education.* San Francisco: Jossey-Bass, 1977.

Cheit, Earl F. "The Benefits and Burdens of Federal Financial Assistance to Higher Education." *American Economic Review,* February 1977, pp. 90–95, and *College Board Review,* Spring 1977, pp. 14–18.

Christoffel, Pamela. "The Government's Lifelong Commitment." *Change,* June 1977, pp. 44–45.

Cooper, Theodore. "Administration Perspectives on Government and Quality of Medical Education." *Journal of Medical Education,* January 1976, pp. 19–22.

Council of Chief State School Officers. *State and Federal Relationships in Education. A Position Statement.* Washington, D.C.: Council of Chief State School Officers, 1971.

Daly, John Charles, et al. *Government and Academia: The Uneasy Bond.* Washington, D.C.: American Enterprise Institute for Public Policy Research, 1978.

Davidson, Robert H., and Stark, Joan S. "The Federal Role." *New Directions for Higher Education,* Spring 1976, pp. 9–23.

Eberly, Donald J. "The Educational Integrity of Community Service and the Need for Federal Support." *New Directions for Higher Education,* Summer 1977, pp. 53–63.

El-Khawas, Elaine H. "Clarifying Roles and Purposes." *New Directions for Higher Education,* Spring 1976, pp. 35–47.

Enarson, Harold L. "The Common Good: Foundation for Partnership." *Educational Record,* vol. 58, no. 2, pp. 123–31.

Federal Interagency Committee on Education. *Keeping your School or College Catalog in Compliance with Federal Laws and Regulations.* Washington, D.C.: Government Printing Office, 1978.

Finn, Chester E., Jr. "Federal Patronage of Universities in the United States: A Rose by Many Other Names?" *Minerva,* Winter 1976–77, pp. 496–529.

Folger, John K. "Building Public Support for Private Higher Education." *Compact,* Summer 1976, pp. 5–9.

Folger, John K., and Orwig, Melvin D. "State Agency Research." *New Directions for Institutional Research,* Winter 1976, pp. 45–56.

Fryer, Thomas W., Jr. "Designing New Personnel Policies: The Permanent Part-Time Faculty Member." *Journal of the College and University Personnel Association,* Spring 1977, pp. 14–21.

Glenny, Lyman A. *State Budgeting for Higher Education: Interagency Conflict and Consensus.* Berkeley: University of California, 1976.

Goodall, Leonard E., ed. *State Politics and Higher Education. A Book of Readings.* Dearborn, Mich.: LMG Associates, 1976.

Gove, Samuel K., and Carpenter, John. "State Lobbying for Higher Education." *Educational Record,* vol. 58, no. 4, pp. 357–72.

Grant, Arthur T., ed. *The Impact of Federal Policies on Higher Education Institutions.* Tucson: University of Arizona, 1977.

Gross, Alan. "Too Old to Teach." *AGB Reports,* September/October 1977, pp. 28–33.

Halperin, Samuel. "Is the Federal Government Taking Over Education?" *Compact,* Summer 1976, pp. 2–4.

Halperin, Samuel. "The Federal Future in Higher Education." *Change,* February 1978, pp. 24–26.

Heyns, Roger W. "Our Best Defense Against Government Regulation." *Educational Record,* vol. 58, no. 4, pp. 350–56.

Hobbs, Walter C., ed. *Government Regulation of Higher Education.* Cambridge, Mass.: Ballinger, 1978.

Hollander, T. Edward. "The View from the State Capital." *Change,* June/July 1978, pp. 43–46.

Hook, Sidney; Kurtz, Paul; and Todorovich, Miro, eds. *The University and the State: What Role for Government in Higher Education?* Buffalo, N.Y.: Prometheus Books, 1978.

Hughes, John F., ed. *Education and the State.* Washington, D.C.: American Council on Education, 1975.

Hughes, John F., and Mills, Olive, eds. *Formulating Policy in Postsecondary Education: The Search for Alternatives.* Washington, D.C.: American Council on Education, 1975.

Hyde, Robert M. "Why Don't Trustees Discuss Government?" *AGB Reports,* January/February 1977, pp. 15–17.

Institute for Educational Leadership. *Federalism at the Crossroads: Improving Educational Policymaking.* Washington, D.C.: George Washington University, 1976.

Johnson, Mark D., and Mortimer, Kenneth P. *Faculty Bargaining and the Politics of Retrenchment in the Pennsylvania State Colleges, 1971–1976.* University Park, Pa.: Pennsylvania State University, 1977.

Kelly, Robert N. "The New Delivery System: A Voice for Caution." *Journal of Student Financial Aid,* February 1977, pp. 35–44.

Klebanoff, Howard M. "Let's Get Legislators and Educators on the Same Team for a Change." *Compact,* Summer 1976, pp. 10–12.

La Noue, George R. "Is the Federal Government Controlling Education? The Federal Tailors." *Education and Urban Society,* February 1977, pp. 197–214.

Latker, Norman J. *University Patent Policy.* Los Angeles: University of Southern California, 1977.

Lawrence, Ben. "The Just Community at What Price?" *College Board Review,* Winter 1977, pp. 16–19, 31–33.

Levin, Nora Jean. "Dilemmas of Disclosure." *New Directions for Higher Education,* Spring 1976, pp. 49–58.

Loftus, Elizabeth. "Follies of Affirmative Action." *Society,* January/February 1977, pp. 21–24.

Lyman, Richard W. "Public Rights and Private Responsibilities: A University Viewpoint." *Journal of Medical Education,* January 1976, pp. 7–13.

Mathews, David. "Changing the Agenda: An Explorer's Map." *AGB Reports,* November/December 1976, pp. 3–6.

Mathews, David et al. *The Changing Agenda for American Higher Education.* Washington, D.C.: Government Printing Office, 1977.

McGill, William J. "The University and the State." *Educational Record,* vol. 58, no. 2, pp. 132–45.

McNamara, William. "Will States' Rights Wrong Education?" *Change,* September 1977, pp. 46–47.

Meisinger, Richard J., Jr. *State Budgeting for Higher Education: The Uses of Formulas.* Berkeley: University of California, 1976.

Miles, Rufus E., Jr. *A Cabinet Department of Education.* Washington, D.C.: American Council on Education, 1976.

Miles, Rufus E., Jr., and McIntyre, Kevin-John H. "A Cabinet Department of Education." *Educational Record,* vol. 57, no. 4, pp. 207–16.

Millett, John D. "External and Other Threats to Institutional Autonomy." *Educational Record,* vol. 58, no. 4, pp. 378–87.

Muller, Steven. "A New American University?" *Daedalus,* Winter 1978, pp. 31–45.

Nicholson, Heather Johnston. "Autonomy and Accountability of Basic Research." *Minerva,* Spring 1977, pp. 32–61.

O'Neil, Robert M. "Federal Forays and Academic Autonomy." *Viewpoints,* September 1976, pp. 73–79.

O'Neil, Robert M. "God and Government at Yale: The Limits of Federal Regulation of Higher Education." *Cincinnati Law Review,* 1975, pp. 525–47.

Phillips, Ione. *The Added Dimension: State and Land-Grant Universities Serving State and Local Government.* Washington, D.C.: National Association of State Universities and Land-Grant Colleges, 1977.

Ribicoff, Abraham A. "A Separate Department of Education: Why Not the Best?" *Change,* February 1978, pp. 27, 63.

Rogers, Paul G. "Congressional Perspectives on Government and Quality of Medical Education." *Journal of Medical Education,* January 1976, pp. 3–6.

Rosenzweig, Robert M. "An End to Autonomy: Who Pulls the Strings?" *Change,* March 1978, pp. 28–34, 62.

Saunders, Charles B., Jr. "Easing the Burden of Federal Regulation: The Next Move Is Ours." *Educational Record,* vol. 57, no. 4, pp. 217–24.

Saunders, Charles B., Jr. "How to Keep the Government from Playing the Featured Role." *Educational Record,* vol. 59, no. 1, pp. 61–69.

Saunders, Charles B., Jr. "Is Regulation Strangulation?" *College Board Review,* Summer 1976, pp. 2–5.

Schotten, Peter and Knight, Gary A. "Effects of the Consumerist Movement on the University." *North Central Association Quarterly,* Spring 1977, pp. 377–84.

Scott, Robert A. "The Hidden Costs of Government Regulations." *Change,* April 1978, pp. 16–23.

Shulman, Carol Herrnstadt. *Keeping Up with Title IX.* Washington, D.C.: American Association for Higher Education, January 1977.

Snyder, Robert. *Federal Policy and Graduate Education.* Washington, D.C.: Federal Interagency Committee on Education, June 1975.

Solomon, Henry, ed. "The Growing Influence of Federal Regulations." *Educational Record,* vol. 58, no. 3, pp. 270–89.

Southern Association of Colleges and Schools. *Colleges and Universities Speak Out on Cost of Federal Compliance in Higher Education.* Atlanta: Southern Association of Colleges and Schools, December 1976.

Stark, Joan S., et al. *The Many Faces of Educational Consumerism.* Lexington, Mass.: Lexington Books, 1977.

"State Regulation of Off-Campus Programs and Out-of-State Institutions." *Issues in Higher Education No. 12*. Atlanta: Southern Regional Education Board, 1978.

Vaughan, George B. "A View from the Trenches." *Community College Frontiers,* Summer 1977, pp. 3–6.

Wabnick, Richard, et al. *Postsecondary Education: The Current Federal Role and Alternative Approaches*. Washington, D.C.: Government Printing Office, 1977.

Webb, LaVarr G., and Marema, Lenore. "God and Mammon: At Brigham Young University, at Wheaton College." *Change,* May 1977, pp. 38–42.

Young, Jerry W. *Accountability Overkill*. Report by American Council on Education Fellow, 1976.

Ziegler, Jerome M., et al. "Dialog: Would State Control of Federal Education Dollars Be More or Less Desirable?" *Change,* October 1976, pp. 50–51.

AMERICAN COUNCIL ON EDUCATION

J. W. PELTASON, *President*

The American Council on Education, founded in 1918 and composed of institutions of higher education and national and regional associations, is the nation's major coordinating body for postsecondary education. Through voluntary and cooperative action, the Council provides comprehensive leadership for improving educational standards, policies, and procedures.